JOY

COMES IN
THE MORNING

JOY
COMES IN
THE MORNING

Psalms for All Seasons

MARK D. FUTATO

PUBLISHING
P.O. BOX 817 • PHILLIPSBURG • NEW JERSEY 08865-0817

Page design and typesetting by Lakeside Design Plus

Printed in the United States of America

Library of Congress Cataloging-in-Publication Data

Futato, Mark David.
    Joy comes in the morning : Psalms for all seasons / Mark D. Futato.
        p. cm.
    Includes bibliographical references and index.
    ISBN 0-87552-718-3
    1. Bible. O. T. Psalms—Criticism, Form. I. Title.

BS1430.52.F87 2004
223'.206—dc22

                                   2004051006

To my children,

Will, Evan, Mark David, and Annie,
with whom I enjoy the journey.

You're the greatest!

Psalm 128:3b–5a

And look at all those children!
There they sit around your table
as vigorous and healthy as young olive trees.
That is the LORD's reward
for those who fear him.
May the LORD continually bless you from Zion.

CONTENTS

Abbreviations

Bible Versions

ESV   English Standard Version
KJV   King James Version
NASB   New American Standard Bible
NIV   New International Version
NKJV   New King James Version
NLT   New Living Translation
NRSV   New Revised Standard Version

Reference Works

HALOT   Ludwig Koehler, Walter Baumgartner, et al., *The Hebrew and Aramaic Lexicon of the Old Testament*. Translated and edited by M. E. J. Richardson et al. 5 vols. Leiden: Brill, 1994–2000.

IBHS   Bruce K. Waltke and M. O'Connor, *An Introduction to Biblical Hebrew Syntax*. Winona Lake, Ind.: Eisenbrauns, 1990.

NIDOTTE Willem A. VanGemeren (ed.), *New International Dictionary of Old Testament Theology and Exegesis*. 5 vols. Grand Rapids: Zondervan, 1997.

TLOT   Ernst Jenni and Claus Westermann (eds.),
          Theological Lexicon of the Old Testament.
          Translated by Mark E. Biddle. 3 vols.
          Peabody, Mass.: Hendrickson, 1997.

TWOT   R. Laird Harris, Gleason L. Archer Jr., and
          Bruce K. Waltke (eds.), *Theological Wordbook
          of the Old Testament*. 2 vols. Chicago: Moody,
          1980.

1 SONGS FOR THE JOURNEY: GENRE IN THE PSALMS

*Let the word of Christ dwell in you richly as you teach
and admonish one another with all wisdom, and as you
sing psalms, hymns and spiritual songs with gratitude
in your hearts to God. (Colossians 3:16 NIV)*

LIFE IS A JOURNEY. Sometimes the sailing is
smooth. Recently the road may have been rough. Along
the way emotions flood our souls. We feel overwhelmed
with sorrow or elated with joy. All sorts of thoughts fill
our minds. We may understand exactly where we are,
or we may be profoundly confused about which direc-
tion to take.

Music makes a difference. Songs can clarify our thinking or release emotions from the deep well of the soul.

I will never forget the Sunday morning that my wife
and I were in church with our children, singing "O

God, our help in ages past, our hope for years to come" at the same time that we were miscarrying our fourth child. As I type the words, "Time, like an ever-rolling stream, bears all its sons away; they fly, forgotten, as a dream dies at the op'ning day," I cannot hold back the tears as I relive the pain of that moment. I am writing in a Borders Book and Music in Winter Park, Florida, wondering what the man sitting at the next table thinks is going on inside me. The words of the song being played in the café reach my conscious mind: "Ain't no mountain high enough, ain't no valley low enough, ain't no river wide enough, to keep me from getting to you" (Marvin Gaye and Tammy Terrell). Sorrow gives way to delight as the music of Motown brings me back to the lighthearted and fun-filled days of junior high. How good God is to give us songs for the journey.

In this chapter we are going to learn about the different kinds of songs that God has given us in the Book of Psalms. God has given us different kinds of songs because we travel on different kinds of terrain in life. I enjoy off-roading in my Jeep Wrangler. Tires that perform well on the smooth highway don't work nearly as well in deep mud. On the other hand, my 33-inch mud-terrain tires are not the most comfortable ride on pavement. So too, the songs written for the good times in life won't work nearly as well in the mire of discouragement. And sad songs just don't fit when we are happy. We naturally turn to happy songs or sad songs in different circumstances. This chapter will give you deeper insight into some of the different kinds of psalms found in the Book of Psalms.

Let's ask a couple of questions that will lead us through a basic introduction to the kinds of songs we find in the Psalms.

What Is Genre?

A genre is a group of writings that have characteristics in common with each other.[1] Without thinking much about it, we group similar writings together. We recognize all stories that begin with "Once upon a time" as fairy tales. We could collect writings that begin with "I am writing in response to last week's article" into a group called letters to the editor. A fairly tale and a letter to the editor are quite different. We would be surprised to read about talking trees in a letter to the editor or about someone's political opinion in a fairy tale. Why? Because each type of literature, each genre, follows its own rules or conventions. Knowing these rules helps us to read with greater understanding.

What is true of literature in general is true of the Bible: the Bible contains different genres. We can divide the Bible into two main genres: prose and poetry. We can then divide poetry into several different genres: for example, psalms, proverbs, and prophetic sermons. Each of these genres has its own "once upon a time," its own rules or conventions. Knowing the conventions, understanding the basic genres of the Psalms, enriches our use of the Psalms.

What Are the Basic Genres?

All of the songs in the Book of Psalms fall into one main genre: they are all psalms. But these songs can be

3

subdivided into separate genres based on characteristics that they have in common. What are the basic kinds of psalms that we are going to encounter when we read the Book of Psalms? Let's look at what I call "the big three."

We could group many of the Psalms into happy psalms or sad psalms and speak of the big two. The happy psalms, however, fall into two distinct groups: those that have recent trouble clearly in view and those that do not. Happy songs without recent personal trouble in view we call *songs of praise*. Sad songs with trouble in view we call *songs of lament*. Songs that express joy because of deliverance from trouble in the recent past we call *songs of thanksgiving*.

While we commonly refer to the big three as *songs of praise*, *songs of lament*, and *songs of thanksgiving*, we can speak of them in another way. In place of songs of praise, lament, and thanksgiving, Walter Brueggemann refers to songs of *orientation, disorientation*, and *reorientation*.[2] By using these labels, Brueggemann shows us something fundamental about how the big three relate to each other and how they relate to the ebb and flow of our lives.

Songs of Praise/Orientation

Songs of praise were composed when everything was going well. They are songs for those trouble-free times in life, times when our lives are well ordered, well oriented. The songs of praise typically celebrate God as Creator and God as Redeemer.

Creation songs of praise often praise God for the orderliness of his creation (Psalm 104). When our lives are well ordered, they are a microcosm of the well-

4

ordered universe. By celebrating God's good creation, we celebrate the goodness of God we are experiencing in life.

When the songs of praise extol God as Redeemer, they are typically celebrating what God has done for us in *the history of his redemptive work*, rather than what God has done for us in our own *personal history*. In Old Testament terms, these psalms celebrate events in the distant past, like the exodus from Egypt (Psalm 105) or the conquest of the promised land (Psalm 47). For Christians, songs of praise celebrate events like the death and resurrection of Christ or the outpouring of the Holy Spirit at Pentecost. By celebrating God's redemptive work in the distant past, we celebrate the faithfulness and reliability of God as the foundation of the good life we are experiencing.

Songs of Lament/Disorientation

We do not always experience life as well ordered. Our lives are not always well oriented. "Disorientation" better describes life at times. The laments or songs of disorientation were written for times such as these.

These are times when you may feel tremendously perplexed or utterly forsaken or paralyzed by fear or overwhelmed with anger or lost in despair. These are times when you cry out, "My God, my God! Why have you forsaken me? Why do you remain so distant? Why do you ignore my cries for help?" (22:1); or, "O LORD, how long will you forget me? Forever? How long will you look the other way? How long must I struggle with anguish in my soul, with sorrow in my heart every day?" (13:1–2); or, "You have taken away my companions and loved ones; only darkness remains" (88:18).

5

The laments are the psalms composed for what some have called the dark night of the soul, for times when "weeping may go on all night" (30:5), perhaps even night after night after night (6:6). The psalms of disorientation give us permission to—and show us how to—let the tears and feelings flow.

Songs of Thanksgiving/Reorientation

Though "weeping may go on all night," says Psalm 30, "joy comes with morning" (30:5). The time eventually comes when you look back at the troublesome days and say to God, "You have turned my mourning into joyful dancing. You have taken away my clothes of mourning and clothed me with joy" (30:11).

You experience God parting the heavens and coming down (144:5) to deliver you from the disorienting trouble that you were in. The songs of thanksgiving express joy and gratitude to God for that deliverance.

Like the songs of praise, the songs of thanksgiving celebrate God's redemptive work. The songs of thanksgiving, however, celebrate God's redemptive work in your own personal history. These psalms thank God for lifting you personally "out of the pit of despair, out of the mud and the mire" and for setting your "feet on solid ground" once again (40:2), for eliminating the chaos and reestablishing good order in your life.

On the path of life there may be stretches when all is well. At other times the going may be pretty rough. The rough road eventually leads to a smooth path once again. God has given us songs for each of these seasons in life: songs of praise, lament, and thanksgiving.

We intuitively turn to the psalms that match our current experience on the path. We don't really need a theoretical understanding of genre to find a psalm that fits our circumstances. What is, therefore, the practical importance to this idea of genre?

Why Is Genre Important?

Why do you need to know about the various genres in the Book of Psalms? Before we answer this question in a couple of ways, let's keep in mind two related considerations. As mentioned earlier, you make genre identifications every time you read a newspaper article or a book. You make these identifications fluently, though unconsciously, just as first-grade children use English fluently, though they have no self-conscious understanding of grammar. In this chapter we are becoming aware of what we have always been doing without being aware of it.

Related to this is the gap between our culture and the ancient culture(s) of the Bible. While we intuitively identify the genre of a piece of literature we read in our own culture, the same intuitions do not work when reading literature from other cultures, like those of the Bible. This is true because literary conventions (rules for writing) change from culture to culture. For example, in our culture quoting what someone said must be done with great precision. If author A is quoting author B, and if author B's work contains a typographical error, our conventions require author A to pass on the misspelling, followed by (sic), so that we know *precisely* who is responsible for the error. The ancient world in general and the Bible in particular were not concerned with such precision in regard to quotations. Their quot-

7

ing was much more like our "giving the gist" of what someone said.

This explains many differences between parallel texts in the Bible, like Matthew 16:25 and Mark 8:35, where the recorded words of Jesus are not precisely the same in both texts:

Matthew 16:25	Mark 8:35
If you try to keep your life for yourself, you will lose it. But if you give up your life for me, you will find true life.	If you try to keep your life for yourself, you will lose it. But if you give up your life for my sake and for the sake of the Good News, you will find true life.

Mark includes the words *and for the sake of the Good News*, while Matthew leaves them out. Both authors *truly* give the gist of what Jesus said without giving us *precisely* what he said.[3]

With these two considerations in mind, let's answer our question as to why genre is important in a couple of ways.

Genre Guides Our Expectations

First of all, genre guides our expectations.[4] For example, when you open a book and read the words *Once upon a time*, you are not surprised if on page two you encounter a tree talking to a little girl. Why no surprise? Why no disbelief? Because the words *Once upon a time* have guided your expectations. Genre determines what you will and will not expect on the following pages. *Once upon a time* indicates that you are reading a fairy tale, and trees talking to little girls is perfectly permissible in this genre.

8

Conversely, if you read the words, "I'm writing in regard to the article that was in the paper last week," and this piece goes on to describe a conversation between a tree and a little girl, you are quite surprised or perplexed or incredulous. Why? Because the opening words have guided your expectations. These words determine what you will and will not allow as believable in what you are reading. "I'm writing in regard to the article that was in the paper last week" indicates that you are reading a letter to the editor, and talking trees are not expected in this genre. Genre guides your expectations.

Let's look at how genre affects our reading of two related stories in the Bible. The first is Judges 9:8–15:

> Once upon a time the trees decided to elect a king. First they said to the olive tree, "Be our king!" But it refused, saying, "Should I quit producing the olive oil that blesses both God and people, just to wave back and forth over the trees?"
>
> Then they said to the fig tree, "You be our king!" But the fig tree also refused, saying, "Should I quit producing my sweet fruit just to wave back and forth over the trees?"
>
> Then they said to the grapevine, "You be our king!" But the grapevine replied, "Should I quit producing the wine that cheers both God and people, just to wave back and forth over the trees?"
>
> Then all the trees finally turned to the thornbush and said, "Come, you be our king!" And the thornbush replied, "If you truly want to make me your king, come and take shelter in my shade. If not, let fire come out from me and devour the cedars of Lebanon."

Though this story is recorded in the Bible, few if any readers would believe that this conversation actually took place in real time and space between real trees and other plants. Why the disbelief? Genre. The NLT correctly discerns the presence of a fable here and clues the English reader in with "Once upon a time." The talking plants are not characters in the narrative itself but are characters in a story being told by a character in the historical narrative. Jotham is telling a fable to make a point—much like Jesus told parables to make a point.

A second text is Numbers 22:28–30, where we read the following conversation between a donkey and a man:

> "What have I done to you that deserves your beating me these three times?" it asked Balaam.
> "Because you have made me look like a fool!" Balaam shouted. "If I had a sword with me, I would kill you!"
> "But I am the same donkey you always ride on," the donkey answered. "Have I ever done anything like this before?"
> "No," he admitted.

Unlike our take on the previous story, we evangelicals affirm that this donkey talked to Balaam in real time and real space. Why the affirmation? Genre. Rather than being a character in a fable being told by a character in the narrative, this donkey is actually one of the characters in the narrative itself. The story of the talking donkey is a historical narrative, not a fable.

Why we believe that the talking trees are not historical and the talking donkey is can be answered in one word: genre. Genre determines what can and cannot be found in a particular piece of literature. Genre is important because genre guides our expectations.

In the following chapters we will study each of the big three genres. We will discover that each genre has its own typical flow of thought. Understanding the typical structure and content of each genre will be a great aid to your understanding of the individual psalms from those genres.

Genre Provides Another Level of Context

Genre is also important because genre provides an additional level of context. Context is essential for interpretation. To put it simply, context determines meaning. The same words in *different contexts* can have completely *different meanings*.

For example, what does the following sentence mean? "That's a bad board." Well, it all depends on the context in which these words are spoken. Imagine that you are at the local lumberyard and you overhear a customer say to a sales representative, "That's a bad board." Here "board" means *lumber* and "bad" means *not good*, as in cracked or crooked. Now imagine that you are at the beach and you overhear one of my sons say to a friend, "That's a bad board." In this context "board" means *surfboard* (made out of Styrofoam and fiberglass, not lumber) and "bad" means *very good*. Same words but different meanings. Why different meanings? Different contexts. Context determines meaning. Context is essential for interpretation. The better we understand the context, the better we understand the text. Genre is one kind of context and so helps us understand the text better.

What does "interpreting in context" mean? It means many things because there are many levels of context.

11

Let's take Psalm 47 as an example. First is the *literary context* provided by the surrounding psalms. In Psalm 46 the nations are in an uproar as they rage against Israel (46:6). Psalm 47 celebrates the subduing of these nations (47:3). And Psalm 48 recounts how the nations were turned back when they attacked Israel (48:4–5).

Second is the *historical context* of the conquest of Canaan, referred to in 47:3–4. The reference to the enemies being put "beneath our feet" (47:3) must be read in the context of Joshua 10:24: "Joshua told the captains of his army, 'Come and put your feet on the kings' necks.' And they did as they were told."

Third is the *cultural context* of the ancient Near East. In the ancient Near East there were many kings. Kings related to each other in a variety of ways. Sometimes, kings were on the same level and related as equals. At other times, one king held a superior position in the relationship. The superior king was the suzerain, and the lesser king was the vassal. The suzerain was known in the ancient Near East as the "Great King." So Psalm 47:3 is not saying that the God of Israel is "a great king." Rather, the psalm affirms that the Lord is the supreme king, "the Great King" of all the earth.

Fourth is the *theological context* of the entire Bible. When Psalm 47 celebrates God's reign as the Great King over the nations, it anticipates the reign of King Jesus. Jesus was born into the royal family of David (Matthew 1:1; Romans 1:3). He was crucified as "King of the Jews" (Luke 23:38). As the risen Lord he is now the "King of kings" who comes to rule the nations (Revelation 19:11–16).

Fifth is the *context provided by genre*. Psalm 47 is a song of praise, so it is helpful to study Psalm 47 in the context of other songs of praise. Psalm 47 is, however, a particular kind of song of praise, one that celebrates the kingship of God. Psalms 93 and 95–99 are also songs of praise that celebrate the kingship of God and are, therefore, helpful in gaining a better understanding of Psalm 47.

Genre is important because it guides our expectations and provides another level of context to deepen our understanding of the text. Genre is important for an additional reason. Genre is a window through which you can look more deeply into the person and work of the Lord Jesus Christ.

What Does Genre Have to Do with Christ?

Let's return for a moment to the text with which I began this chapter:

> Let the word of Christ dwell in you richly as you teach and admonish one another with all wisdom, and as you sing psalms, hymns and spiritual songs with gratitude in your hearts to God. (Colossians 3:16 NIV)

The Apostle Paul encourages us to let "the word of Christ" saturate our lives by singing "psalms, hymns and spiritual songs." The Greek words that Paul uses for "psalms," "hymns," and "songs" are all used in the ancient Greek translation of the Old Testament that Paul would have used. These three words are used in the titles to various psalms.[5] So while "the word of Christ" includes more than the Psalms, the Psalms are "the word of Christ." "The word of Christ" here would mean "the word spoken about Christ" in the first place and "the word spoken by Christ" in the second place.

13

When reading a psalm, it is helpful to read that psalm as speaking about Christ and to read it as being spoken by Christ.[6] Each of these perspectives will yield different insights into any given psalm. We can use these two perspectives for the simple reason that, as the second person of the Trinity, Christ is the Lord of the covenant to whom the Psalms are addressed by us and, as the Messiah, Christ is the servant of the covenant by whom the Psalms are voiced for us.

Each of the genres we are studying—songs of praise, lament, and thanksgiving—are different windows through which we can look to gain perspective on who Jesus is and what he has done for us. While the "about Christ" and "by Christ" perspectives help with each of these genres, the songs of praise lend themselves to the "about Christ" perspective, and the songs of lament and the songs of thanksgiving lend themselves to the "by Christ" perspective.

The study of genre is, therefore, not a sterile exercise. By learning to read the various psalms in keeping with their genres, you are going to see more of the richness of Christ, so that this richness will fill your life more and more.

Christ and Our Songs of Praises

Two major themes in the songs of praise are the praise of God as our Creator and the praise of God as our Redeemer. For example, Psalm 104:1, 24 praises God as our Creator:

> Praise the LORD, I tell myself;
> O LORD my God, how great you are! . . .

O LORD, what a variety of things you have made!
In wisdom you have made them all.
The earth is full of your creatures.

And 107:1–2 praises God as our Redeemer:

Give thanks to the LORD, for he is good!
His faithful love endures forever.
Has the LORD redeemed you? Then speak out!
Tell others he has saved you from your enemies.

The New Testament presents Christ as both our Creator and our Redeemer. The Apostle John says that Jesus

created everything there is. Nothing exists that he
didn't make. (John 1:3)

And the Apostle Paul says that

Christ *redeemed* us from the curse of the law by
becoming a curse for us, for it is written: "Cursed is
everyone who is hung on a tree." (Galatians 3:13 NIV)

So when we sing or read the songs of praise we are singing and reading about Christ our Creator, our Redeemer, our Shepherd, our King, our God.

Christ and Our Songs of Lament

David once cried out in agony:

My God, my God! Why have you forsaken me?
Why do you remain so distant?
Why do you ignore my cries for help? (22:1)

15

Many of us have shared David's thoughts and feelings along the path of life. While we may have felt terribly alone, we were never truly alone in those times, because Jesus was there with us. Jesus no doubt prayed the laments throughout his journey on this earth, as the author of Hebrews says:

> While Jesus was here on earth, he offered prayers and pleadings, with a loud cry and tears, to the one who could deliver him out of death. (Hebrews 5:7)

And Jesus prayed the laments most intensely on the cross, as Matthew says:

> At about three o'clock, Jesus called out with a loud voice, "*Eli, Eli, lema sabachthani?*" which means, "My God, my God, why have you forsaken me?" (Matthew 27:46)

So, when we sing or read the laments, we are singing and reading about Christ, who has gone before us and sung the laments for us.

Christ and Our Songs of Thanksgiving

Hebrews 5:7 tells us:

> While Jesus was here on earth, he offered prayers and pleadings, with a loud cry and tears, to the one who could deliver him out of death. *And God heard his prayers* because of his reverence for God.

God heard Jesus' agonizing cry on the cross and redeemed him from death and hell by raising him from the dead. Jesus no doubt celebrated this deliverance with songs of thanksgiving. The author of Hebrews leads us to this conclusion, when he quotes Jesus as saying to the Father:

> I will declare the wonder of your name to my brothers and sisters.
> I will praise you among all your people.
> (Hebrews 2:12)

Here Jesus is reciting the words of thanksgiving, first recorded in Psalm 22:22. From this text we learn not only that Jesus sang the songs of thanksgiving for us, but also that he now leads us as we too thank God for all that he has done and continues to do for us in answer to our prayers.

Understanding the genres of the Psalms guides your expectations, provides you an additional level of context, and gives you multiple windows through which you can look more deeply into who Jesus is and what he has done and continues to do for you. And this emphasis on Christ is by no means an exclusion of the Father and the Spirit. Rather, our focus on the Son in the Psalms is to the glory of the Father through the power of the Spirit, as the New Testament says:

> Don't be drunk with wine, because that will ruin your life. Instead, *let the Holy Spirit fill and control you.* Then you *will sing psalms and hymns and spiritual songs* among yourselves, making music to the Lord in your hearts. And you will always *give thanks for everything to God the Father* in *the name of our Lord Jesus Christ.* (Ephesians 5:18–20)

17

2 WHAT A WONDERFUL WORLD! THE SONGS OF PRAISE

Praise the Lord, I tell myself;
O Lord my God, how great you are!
You are robed with honor and with majesty;
you are dressed in a robe of light.
You stretch out the starry curtain of the heavens;
you lay out the rafters of your home in the rain
clouds.
You make the clouds your chariots;
you ride upon the wings of the wind.
The winds are your messengers;
flames of fire are your servants.

You placed the world on its foundation
so it would never be moved.
You clothed the earth with floods of water,
water that covered even the mountains.
At the sound of your rebuke, the water fled;
at the sound of your thunder, it fled away.

Mountains rose and valleys sank
to the levels you decreed.
Then you set a firm boundary for the seas,
so they would never again cover the earth.

You make the springs pour water into ravines,
so streams gush down from the mountains.
They provide water for all the animals,
and the wild donkeys quench their thirst.
The birds nest beside the streams
and sing among the branches of the trees.
You send rain on the mountains from your heavenly
home,
and you fill the earth with the fruit of your labor.
You cause grass to grow for the cattle.
You cause plants to grow for people to use.
You allow them to produce grain from the earth, [1]
wine to make them glad,
and olive oil to make them healthy—
all the foods that give people strength.
The trees of the LORD are well cared for—
the cedars of Lebanon that he planted.
There the birds make their nests,
and the storks make their homes in the firs.
High in the mountains are pastures for the wild goats,
and the rocks form a refuge for rock badgers.
You made the moon to mark the seasons
and the sun that knows when to set.
You send the darkness, and it becomes night,
when all the forest animals prowl about.
Then the young lions roar for their food,
but they are dependent on God.

At dawn they slink back
into their dens to rest.
Then people go off to their work;
they labor until the evening shadows fall again.

O LORD, what a variety of things you have made!
In wisdom you have made them all.
The earth is full of your creatures.
Here is the ocean, vast and wide,
teeming with life of every kind,
both great and small.
See the ships sailing along,
and Leviathan, which you made to play in the sea.
Every one of these depends on you
to give them their food as they need it.
When you supply it, they gather it.
You open your hand to feed them, and they are
satisfied.
But if you turn away from them, they panic.
When you take away their breath, they die
and turn again to dust.
When you send your Spirit, new life is born
to replenish all the living of the earth.

May the glory of the LORD last forever!
The LORD rejoices in all he has made!
The earth trembles at his glance;
the mountains burst into flame at his touch.
I will sing to the LORD as long as I live.
I will praise my God to my last breath!
May he be pleased by all these thoughts about him,
for I rejoice in the LORD.

21

Let all sinners vanish from the face of the earth;
  let the wicked disappear forever.
As for me—I will praise the LORD!

Praise the LORD! *(Psalm 104 NLT modified)*

FOR THE FIRST thirteen years of our marriage, my wife and I walked on a pretty smooth path in life. We encountered small bumps along the way, of course, but faced no major obstacles in this season of our life. No major crises. No struggles of faith. Just a long stretch of relatively trouble-free living.

Many of us experience times like this. The smooth stretches may be shorter or longer, more or less frequent, but when we are on them life is like a placid lake on a fresh spring morning. The songs of praise found in the Book of Psalms paint pictures of life at such times. The songs of praise capture the melody of life when we think to ourselves, "What a wonderful world!"

A bright, positive mood characterizes the songs of praise. The chaotic side of life lies in the distant background in these psalms. The foreground, on the other hand, is filled with faith—faith in the goodness and faithfulness of God, faith that the world in which we live will be experienced as good day after good day because God governs all. So the key word of the songs of praise is "praise." The songs of praise exalt God for life, life that is good.

The songs of praise tend to focus on God's works of creation and providence (Psalm 29) or his work of redemption (Psalm 47). The songs of praise affirm that God has created and continues to maintain a well-

22

ordered world where life abounds (Psalm 65). And when the psalmist brings redemption into view, he describes with broad strokes and in general terms God's redemptive work in the past that has established a good life in the present (Psalm 146).

The songs of praise usually fall into three sections: an opening invitation to praise God, a central delineation of the praiseworthy character and actions of God, and a concluding affirmation of faith or reinvitation to praise and worship.

Songs of praise invite all to the concert of praise. On the smallest scale, for example, David in Psalm 103 invites himself to praise the Lord:

> Praise the Lord, *I tell myself*;
>   with my whole heart, *I will praise* his holy name.
> Praise the Lord, *I tell myself*,
>   and never forget the good things he does for me.

Sometimes the psalmist broadens the invitation to the congregation, as in Psalm 118:

> Give thanks to the Lord, for he is good!
>   His faithful love endures forever.
> Let *the congregation* of Israel repeat:
>   "His faithful love endures forever."

At other times, the psalmist expands the invitation even further to include all the nations. Thus Psalm 117, the shortest psalm, begins:

> Praise the Lord, all you *nations*.
>   Praise him, all you *people of the earth*.

23

On several occasions, Psalm 29 being one, the psalmist transcends the earth to enlist the angels of heaven in the praise of God:

> Give honor to the LORD, you *angels*;
> give honor to the LORD for his glory and strength.
> Give honor to the LORD for the glory of his name.
> Worship the LORD in the splendor of his holiness.

In unmatched exuberance Psalm 148 calls the whole created realm to join the chorus. Psalm 148:1–6 addresses heaven and its countless hosts:

> Praise the LORD from *the heavens*.

And 148:7–14 summons every part of the terrestrial globe—animate and inanimate—to worship the God who has created and maintains this wonderful world:

> Praise the LORD from *the earth*.

Psalm 148:13 captures the whole as well as any one verse can:

> Let them all praise the name of the LORD.
> For his name is very great;
> his glory towers over the *earth and heaven*!

The central section of each song of praise provides you with motivation to praise or the actual substance of praise by recalling who God is and what he has done. Praise is the acknowledgement or confession of God's attributes and actions.[2] The closest thing to a definition of "praise" is found in 34:1–3, where David says:

I will *praise* the LORD at all times. . . .
Come, let us *tell of* the LORD's *greatness*.

To praise is to tell others just how great the Lord is in terms of who he is and what he has done. Psalm 34 amplifies the greatness of God in terms of how God answers prayer (34:6) because God is so good (34:8):

I cried out to the LORD in my suffering, and *he heard me.* . . .
Taste and see that *the LORD is good*.

Other songs of praise focus on other attributes and actions of God, as we will now see.

This central section frequently takes up most of the space in the songs of praise and brings a variety of themes into focus. Psalmists often introduce these themes with the Hebrew word *ki*, which can be translated "for" or "because." Here are just a few examples. Psalm 30 draws our attention to the healing mercy of God:

I will praise you, LORD, *for* [*ki*] you have rescued me. . . .
O LORD my God, I cried out to you for help,
and *you restored my health*.

Psalm 47 highlights the kingship of God:

Come, everyone, and clap your hands for joy!
Shout to God with joyful praise!
For [*ki*] the LORD Most High is awesome.
He is *the great King* of all the earth.

Psalm 117:1–2 focuses on the unfailing love of God:

25

> Praise the LORD, all you nations.
> Praise him, all you people of the earth.
> *For* [*ki*] he loves us with *unfailing love.*

God's delight in us is the theme of praise in Psalm 149:

> Praise the LORD!
> Sing to the LORD a new song.
> Sing his praises in the assembly of the faith-
> ful. . . .
> *For* [*ki*] the LORD *delights* in his people.

In their central sections the songs of praise provide us with an abundance of reasons for giving praise to the Lord.

In keeping with the positive tone of the first two sections, the songs of praise come to a conclusion on an equally positive note. Quite frequently, the conclusion contains a repeated call to praise, as in Psalm 103:

> *Praise the LORD*, you angels of his,
> you mighty creatures who carry out his plans,
> listening for each of his commands.
> Yes, *praise the LORD*, you armies of angels
> who serve him and do his will!
> *Praise the LORD*, everything he has created,
> everywhere in his kingdom.
> As for me—I, too, will *praise the LORD.*

Matching the first two lines of this song of praise, the last line calls David himself to praise the Lord.[3] This conclusion, however, extends beyond David and invites the angels and in fact the whole created realm to join the concert of praise.

The songs of praise may also come to a close with a strong affirmation of faith and confidence in the Lord, as is the case in Psalm 29, which affirms that the Lord is in control of the world and this control will result in great blessing:

> The LORD *rules* over the floodwaters.
> The LORD *reigns* as king forever.
> The LORD *gives* his people *strength*.
> The LORD *blesses* them with *peace*.

Now that we are oriented to the typical flow of a song of praise, let's follow the course as we study the quintessential creation song of praise, Psalm 104.

Psalm 104 praises the Lord for creating and preserving the wonderful world in which we live. Through this psalm the poet takes us on a cosmic field trip during which we will experience a universe that is shining with the Creator's majesty (104:1–2a), teeming with the Creator's wisdom (104:2b–26), overflowing with the Creator's generosity (104:27–30), and glowing with the Creator's glory (104:31–35).

Shining with the Creator's Majesty (Psalm 104:1–2a)

Like Psalm 103, Psalm 104 opens with a summons to the self to praise the Lord: "Praise the LORD, I tell myself." The psalmist's reflections on creation are intensely personal. Though we may at times feel like a speck of cosmic dust in a meaningless and impersonal universe, Psalm 104 assures us that at the very heart of this wonderful world is relationship—relationship between the individual self and the Creator of the galaxies. We are never alone. The God who created the universe in the deep recesses of time and space is present today—present in great majesty, present with infinite wisdom, present with infinite generosity, present in great glory, present to receive personally the praise offered by a single soul who experiences this God in this wonderful world.

Majesty is the key characteristic of God in this opening stanza of Psalm 104. The psalmist invites you to look at the world that God has made and to see God's royal and resplendent majesty everywhere.

Royal Majesty (Psalm 104:1)

Why do I say that this is a royal majesty or the majesty of a king? Two reasons. The first is found in the affirmation that God is "great":

O LORD my God, how *great* you are!

Just as we use the word *majesty* in association with royalty when we refer to the Queen of England as "Her Majesty," the ancient Hebrews used the word *great* in association with royalty. Psalm 47:2 refers to God as "the great King." In the same way 95:3 refers to the Lord as "the great King." In the context of the ancient world at large, this expression would be better translated as "the Great King," since it is almost a technical phrase used to refer to the king who reigns supreme over all other kings and kingdoms. This is why the full text of 95:3 reads:

For the LORD is a great God,
    the great King *above all gods*.

In saying that God is "great," Psalm 104 shouts the praise of the King of kings and Lord of lords. This interpretation is confirmed by the pair "honor and majesty." Honor and majesty are regularly associated with royalty in the Book of Psalms. God dresses the *human king* with "honor/splendor⁴ and majesty" in 21:5:

> Your victory brings him [the human king] great honor,
> and you have clothed him with splendor and majesty.⁵

In the same way, the *divine King* is "robed with honor and with majesty" in 104:1. The image is that of God dressed in the magnificent regalia of a reigning monarch. The point is that God's creating and governing of the universe was and is the activity of a king. Another psalmist makes this same point in another song of praise, 111:3: "Everything he does reveals his *glory and majesty.*"

God's creation speaks to you in a very personal way. The creation tells you that God is here. He is here as the Great King in all his splendor and majesty. He is here to receive your praise as you live in his wonderful world.

Resplendent Majesty (Psalm 104:2a)

"Light" is used in reference to God nine times in the Book of Psalms. While it is not possible to exhaust the meaning of "you are dressed in a robe of light" (104:2a), we can draw out four dimensions of this image as it is used in this psalm.⁶

First, light is an image of God's transcendence and immanence—God's distance from us and God's closeness to us. As the source of physical sunlight is out there—outside the earthly sphere—so God is "out there"—transcending or going beyond the limits of the created realm. As sunlight permeates the earth, so God permeates every inch of earthly space and every second of earthly time. Psalm 104 images for us a God whose "home" is far above us (104:3, 13) and who at the same time is so close to us that he feeds us right from the palm of his hand (104:28). The infinite God whom we cannot know exhaustively is the personal God whom we can know truly.

Second, light is an image of God's glory. God's glory is, among other things, the visible and radiant manifestation of God's holy character.[7] The connection between holiness and glory is seen in Isaiah 6:3:

Holy, holy, holy is the LORD Almighty!
The whole earth is filled with his *glory*!

God's glory is typically "seen" as "radiant splendor" in the Old Testament. Moses said to God, "Now *show* me your glory" (Exodus 33:18 NIV). The glory of God on Mount Sinai "looked like a devouring fire" (24:17). To describe God's glory Ezekiel uses images of lightning, brilliant light, fire, glowing metal, coals of fire, brilliant torches, sparkling crystal, blue sapphire, and shining splendor (Ezekiel 1). In keeping with this, the Apostle John says of Jesus that "the Word became human. . . . And we have *seen his glory*" (John 1:14). And with imagery reminiscent of Ezekiel, John says that the New Jerusalem "*shone with the glory* of God, and its *brilliance* was like that of a very *precious jewel*, like a *jasper*, clear as *crystal*" (Revelation 21:11 NIV). In the remainder of

Psalm 104, the poet will show us the glory of God as it can be seen in every nook and cranny of the creation. Third, light is an image of God's rule. By referring to God "dressed . . . in light" the psalmist continues the image of God as king "robed with honor and majesty." The connection between light and rule is obvious in the creation account, where we read that "God made two great *lights*—the greater *light* to *govern* the day and the lesser *light* to *govern* the night" (Genesis 1:16 NIV). God also said that "the person who *rules* righteously . . . is like the *light* of the morning, like the sunrise bursting forth in a cloudless sky" (2 Samuel 23:3–4). Psalm 104 shows us a transcendent God who is present throughout the creation in all his glory to rule over the creation he has made.

Fourth, light is an image of God's order. The rule of God establishes and maintains a life-giving order in the world. Darkness is associated with chaos in the Bible. In the beginning the "earth was empty, a formless mass cloaked in darkness," according to Genesis 1:2. God's first royal action to bring order into the world was the creation of light. The picture of God "dressed in a robe of light" in Psalm 104:2 fits a psalm that accentuates God's royal work of creating and maintaining a well-ordered world that manifests the wisdom of God. To this wise order in the world we, with the psalmist, now turn.

Teeming with the Creator's Wisdom (Psalm 104:2b–26)

> O LORD, what a variety of things you have made!
> *In wisdom you have made them all.* (104:24)

Every aspect of this diverse creation bears witness to the wisdom of the Creator.[8] Psalm 104:2b–26 focuses our attention on four dimensions of creation to illustrate for us how the whole creation is teeming with this wisdom. Each dimension reveals an amazing order in the universe. This order, which is the foundation of life, manifests the wisdom of God.

Wisdom in the Structure of the Universe (Psalm 104:2b–9)

Sometimes the Bible paints a picture of the universe in three layers: "heaven above . . . the earth beneath . . . the water under the earth" (Exodus 20:4 NASB). At other times, as in Psalm 104:2b–9, the picture has only two layers: the upper layer, or the heavens (104:2b–4), and the lower layer, or the earth and sea (104:5–9). This two-layered perspective of Psalm 104 reveals the order-creating wisdom of God.

The heavens are the dwelling place of the transcendent God of light. Two different images are used to show us this. One image portrays the heavens as a tent: "You stretch out the starry curtain of the heavens." The Hebrew word translated "curtain" in the NLT is frequently used for the tent/tabernacle in which God dwelled before the building of the temple (see Exodus 26, where the NLT uses the word *sheet*). As God dwelled in a tent/tabernacle on earth, so God dwells in the tent of heaven (see Isaiah 40:22). When you look up on a cloudless day and see the blue expanse above, do you see the inside of a vast tent stretched out above you? This is what the poet invites you to see, and then he wishes you to remember that the God of light dwells in heaven and rules from there.

The second image is that of a solid house: "He lays the beams of His upper chambers in the waters" (Psalm 104:3 NASB). The "waters" here are "the waters which were above the expanse" in Genesis 1:7 (NASB). As a house built on wet ground needs a solid foundation, so God's heavenly dwelling, his "upper chambers" built on the waters above, need a solid foundation in this image that the poet is painting for us. The waters on which God's celestial home are founded are the source from which the Creator and King will dispense the rains needed for life on the earth. So the poet moves on to speak of rain clouds.

As ancient kings rode on chariots, so God as King is pictured with his royal retinue riding on chariots: "You make the clouds your chariots" (Psalm 104:3). God's chariots are not, however, made of wood and metal. Rather, God's chariots are the rain clouds (for other images of God riding on clouds, see Deuteronomy 33:26; Psalm 68:4; Isaiah 19:1). The Hebrew word translated "clouds" is a typical Hebrew word for "rain clouds" (77:17; 147:8). When ancient Israelites saw rain clouds approaching, they saw the approach of their divine King, coming to provide all that they needed for life (Deuteronomy 33:26). What do you see? Just rain clouds? Or chariots? In the winds that carry the clouds that bring the rain, do you sense the presence of the heavenly retinue (Psalm 104:4) or just the moving of air?

Whether you are gazing at the blue expanse of the sky or watching rain clouds on the horizon or feeling the wind that is the harbinger of rain, you are experiencing the wonderful order that God built into the universe with his great wisdom. You are experiencing a wonderful part of the wonderful world that God made for you to enjoy.

The lower layer of the universe equally manifests the orderly wisdom of the Creator. As God's heavenly dwelling needed a foundation, having been built on the celestial waters, so humanity's earthly dwelling needed a secure foundation (104:5), because it, too, was built on water in the imagery of the Psalms:

> The earth is the LORD's, and everything in it.
> The world and all its people belong to him.
> *For he laid the earth's foundation on the seas*
> *and built it on the ocean depths.* (24:1–2)

In the beginning, before God's wise order was fully established, water covered the whole earth (Genesis 1:2–8). Psalm 104 describes this situation in these words: "You clothed the earth with floods of water, water that covered even the mountains" (104:6). This is not a wonderful world, at least not from the perspective of a world intended for human life as we know it. So God brought life-providing order into this watery chaos by gathering the waters that covered the earth into one place—the sea—so that dry land could appear (Genesis 1:9). The description of this scenario in Psalm 104 is more dramatic: God's thunderous rebuke drives the waters off the land, and as the mountains rise, the waters rush down through the valleys to their proper place—the sea—where they are required to remain so as never again to inhibit life on earth (104:7–9).

I have had the privilege of living near an ocean since 1988. I love the beach, where land and sea meet. I enjoy watching the ebb and flow of the tide. The waves come further and further up onto the shore, but they always halt their advance and retreat for a while. All of this is part of God's wonderful order for life in this world. With the heavens above and the earth and sea below, the basic structures of a well-ordered universe are in place. The earth began its existence inundated by water. At this point in the developing story line of Psalm 104, there is no water on the earth, as all of the waters are contained either above the vault of the heavens or behind the boundary of the shoreline. No water on earth would mean no life. From where will the waters come that are so necessary for life?

Wisdom in the Provision of Water (Psalm 104:10–18)

An earth with *no* water is as inhospitable as an earth *covered* with water. So God in great wisdom provided (and provides) water for the land from both terrestrial and celestial sources.

The provision of groundwater first occupies the poet in 104:10–12. The psalmist mentions the two primary sources of groundwater in ancient Israel: springs and streams (104:10). Psalm 74:15 also mentions the creation of these two water sources:

> You caused the springs and streams to gush forth.

In God's economy, these springs and streams not only provide water to quench the thirst of all the animals (104:11) but they also create an environment for the lodging of wildlife (104:12). What a wonderful world!

35

Ancient Israelites knew that there was a connection between the terrestrial water and the celestial water. They knew that without rain springs dry up and streams cease to flow. They also knew that water was needed for life where springs and streams could not provide that water. So the poet moves on in 104:13–18 to describe God's provision of the rains without which life in Israel was impossible. The psalmist says of the Creator, "You send rain on the mountains from your heavenly home" (104:13a). The word for "heavenly home" is the same word used back in 104:3, where the psalmist described the founding of God's heavenly house on the celestial waters. As the Creator and King, God lovingly releases the celestial waters in the form of rain to fructify the earth: "You fill the earth with the fruit of your labor" (104:13b).

These rains provide water for the grasses needed by the herbivores (104:14a) and the agricultural produce needed by humans (104:14b). The three primary agricultural products in ancient Israel were grain, grapes, and olives (see note 1 above). Old Testament authors frequently refer to this triad in this order, because this is the order in which these crops are harvested (see, e.g., Deuteronomy 7:13; 2 Chronicles 32:28; Jeremiah 31:12). So when the prophet wants to speak of God's generosity, he says, "Look! I am sending you grain and wine and olive oil, enough to satisfy your needs" (Joel 2:19).

The rains also provide the water needed for the mountainous regions of the land (Psalm 104:16–18). The Creator not only "planted" the trees of the mountains, but he also well cares for these trees by providing them all the rain they need to thrive (104:16). The well-watered trees in turn provide lodging for birds (104:17). The rains also provide the high mountain pastures for the likes of wild goats and rock badgers (104:18).

All of this marvelous order, seen in the Creator's provision of the groundwaters and rains that result in teeming life on earth, teaches us about the wisdom of our Creator and the wonderful world he has made for us.

Wisdom in the Rhythm of the Day
(Psalm 104:19–23)

The marvelous order instituted by the Creator is also evident in the rhythm of night and day (Genesis 1:3–5). While the moon and sun have a variety of jobs in the creation, their primary task in the mind of the psalmist is to govern the night and the day respectively. Psalm 104:19 provides a synopsis or summary of the rhythm of the day by mentioning the creation of the moon first and then the sun. The poet then expands on this synopsis by describing the activities of the night (104:20–21) and then those of the day (104:22–23). The *artistic order* of 104:19–23 serves to underscore the *theology of order* being set forth by the poet.[9]

From the perspective of this poem the darkness of night carries no ominous overtones.[10] The darkness provides certain wild animals the cover that they need to hunt for their prey. In the eye of the poet, the night is a beautiful time, for it is the time when the lions "seek their food from God" (104:21 NIV). God is present in the darkness to care for the creatures he has made. The darkness of night is part of the wonderful world that God made.

In the Creator's order, the dawning of the day is a signal for the wild animals to return to their dens (104:22) and for humans to rise to their labor (104:23). Humans engage in their activities throughout the day. This is God's design for a wonderful world. Humans go about their business "until the evening," after which they return to their homes to rest and the wild animals emerge for another night of life. There is a time and a place for all in God's wonderful world.

Wisdom in the Vastness of the Sea (Psalm 104:24–26)

The poet gives the sea little treatment (three verses) in comparison with the land (nineteen verses). This is probably because the ancient Israelites were not a seafaring people; the Mediterranean coast line of Israel had no natural harbors. When, for example, King Solomon built a fleet of ships, he sailed them from Elath on the Gulf of Aqaba and used Phoenician crews supplied by King Hiram of Tyre (1 Kings 9:26–28).

The poet does not view the sea as a place of danger and death, as is sometimes the case in the Old Testament. The sea is rather a playground (Psalm 104:26) that is "teeming with life of every kind" (104:25):

> O LORD, what a variety of things you have made!
> In wisdom you have made them all.
> The earth is full of your creatures. (104:24)

The heavens (104:2b–4), earth (104:5–23), sea (104:24–26), winds (104:4), mountains (104:8), shoreline (104:9), springs (104:10–12), rain (104:13–18), night (104:20–21), day (104:22–23), birds (104:12), cattle (104:14), rock badgers (104:18), lions (104:21), fish (104:25–26), grass (104:14), cedars (104:16), humans (104:23), and more—what a wonderful world God has made!

Overflowing with the Creator's Generosity (Psalm 104:27–30)

The wonderful world that God made reveals to the eyes of faith both the majesty (104:1–2a) and the wisdom (104:2b–26) of the Creator. What's more, this wonderful word gives us a glimpse into the Creator's heart. When we gaze into the heart of God through the lens of this psalm, we see a heart overflowing with generosity toward all that God has made. Inseparably bound to the generosity of God is his intimate, personal involvement that comes to light in 104:27–30. Let's look at four aspects of the Creator's generosity.

Timely Generosity (Psalm 104:27)

> These all look to you
> to give them their food at the proper time. (NIV)

Here the poet uses a modified form of zeugma. Zeugma is a figure of speech that uses language in reference to two or more entities, though the language makes sense in relation to only one of the entities. God's "giving food" makes sense only in reference to the animals and humans previously mentioned, but is applied by the psalmist to "all," that is, to the whole of the creation. The point of the figure is that the Creator knows just the right time to pour out his generous bounty on every aspect of the creation. We may at times think that God is too slow or too late in providing us what we need, but God exercises a timely care for the whole creation, including us. God provides everything "at the proper time."

Satisfying Generosity (Psalm 104:28)

When you supply it, they gather it.
You open your hand to feed them, and they are
satisfied.

The use of zeugma continues in 104:28. This verse, perhaps better than any verse in the Bible, shows the personal and intimate care God takes of the creation. God is portrayed as bending down to feed creatures from the palm of his hand. This is no mechanical and impersonal world in which we live. We live in a wonderful world permeated by the personal presence of the Creator. This presence is a generous presence that satisfies our deepest desires.

Sovereign Generosity (Psalm 104:29)

But if you turn away from them, they panic.
When you take away their breath, they die
and turn again to dust.

Hannah had it right when she said, "The LORD brings both death and life; he brings some down to the grave but raises others up" (1 Samuel 2:6). Ecclesiastes reminds us that all humans and animals eventually return to the dust from which they came (Ecclesiastes 3:20). David once confessed to God, "My times are in your hands" (Psalm 31:15 NIV). God's generous gift of life is a sovereign gift. This gift does not last forever in its current form, and so life is not to be taken for granted but is to be enjoyed in great gratitude each day that we have in this wonderful world.

Renewable Generosity (Psalm 104:30)

> When you send your Spirit,
>   they are created,
>   and you renew the face of the earth. (NIV)

It is interesting that the sequence is death (104:29) followed by life (104:30). While death is part of our experience in this world, death does not get the last word. The Spirit, who was present in the beginning (Genesis 1:2) to bring teeming life into the dark void, is still present to bring renewed life—even in the wake of death. Like God's love and compassion (Lamentations 3:23), God's generous gift of life is renewed every day.

In a poem that celebrates God's gift of rain to ancient farmers (104:3, 13–18), the renewing of the face of the earth (104:30) no doubt refers to the coming of the fall rains to end the dry season (104:29) and begin a new agricultural year. Just as ancient Israelites eagerly awaited the renewal of God's generosity in the coming of the fall rains, we too can look to God to renew his generosity to us when we experience a "dry season," be it spiritual, physical, financial, emotional, relational, or any other form of "drought." God's generosity is not only timely, satisfying, and sovereign, it is also always renewable.

Glowing with the Creator's Glory (Psalm 104:31–35)

The magnificent song of praise to the Creator of such a wonderful world culminates in a crescendo of worship. This worship finds its focus on the Creator's glory (104:31a), a theme that is a fitting closure to a poem that

41

opens with a picture of God "robed with honor and with majesty" (104:1). The glory of the Creator is accompanied by rejoicing (104:31b, 34b), singing (104:33a), making music (104:33b), and praising (104:35). So let's find out what the Creator's "glory" means and then experience the joy and praise that flows from this glory.

The Meaning of God's Glory (Psalm 104:31a, 32, 35a)

> May the glory of the LORD last forever! (104:31a)

The Hebrew word for glory is *kavod*, and like most words *kavod* is used in a variety of ways in the Hebrew Bible. The noun *kavod* has three distinct but related senses: (1) a person's *personal accomplishments* (2) that are the basis of this person's *own honor* (3) and the basis of the *honor paid* to this person by other people.[11] In any one context only one of these three senses will be primary, though the other two are probably present.

Which is the sense in 104:31? Since the second half of a poetic line often adds something to the first half, like an explanation, perhaps the second half of the verse can guide us to the proper sense of "glory" in this text. The "glory of the LORD" lasting forever is followed by the Lord rejoicing in "all he has made." So the Lord's "glory" is best understood as his "accomplishments," in particular this wonderful world he has made. Psalm 19:1 uses "glory" in this exact same way:

> The heavens tell of the glory of God.
> The skies display his marvelous craftsmanship.

42

Here God's "glory" is God's "craftsmanship." The Hebrew word translated "craftsmanship" is the same word translated "all he has made" in Psalm 104. So, "May the glory of the LORD last forever" is another way of saying, "May the LORD's glorious creation last forever" or "May the creation that manifests the LORD's glory last forever."[12]

Joined with this prayer is the seemingly odd request of 104:35:

> Let all sinners vanish from the face of the earth;
> let the wicked disappear forever.

How are we to understand this request? Here is one possibility. The presence of "sinners" and "the wicked" (104:35a) might move the Lord to come in judgment, causing the earth to "tremble at his glance" and the mountains to "burst into flame at his touch" (104:32). The psalmist desires the removal of all possible reasons for such a coming of the Lord. The psalmist desires the continuance of this wonderful world that manifests the glory of the Creator, because if the glorious creation does not continue, neither will the great joy and the great praise that are to fill this wonderful world.

The Joy of God's Glory (Psalm 104:31b, 34)

> The LORD rejoices in all he has made. . . .
> I rejoice in the LORD.

God's glorious creation results in great joy: great joy for God and great joy for us. Psalm 104:31b says, "The LORD rejoices in all he has made!" An ancient sage tells us that the Creator's Wisdom was filled with delight during the entire creative process, "rejoicing in his whole world and delighting in mankind" (Proverbs 8:31 NIV). God was certainly not emotionless when at the end of that process he "looked over all he had made, and he saw that it was excellent in every way" (Genesis 1:31). He was no doubt filled with great joy. And God still derives great joy from the creation, just as an artist derives great joy from a masterpiece. This wonderful world is a source of great joy for God.

As the Lord rejoices in the creation (Psalm 104:31b), the psalmist rejoices in the Lord (104:34). In context this must mean that the psalmist rejoices in the Lord as Creator. How so? By rejoicing in the Lord's creation. While distinct, joy in the creation and joy in the Creator could not be separated in the experience of ancient Israelites. When the ancients looked into the sky and saw clouds, they saw the Creator's chariot (104:3). In the wind and lightning they perceived God's messengers (104:4). At the seashore they delighted in God's order (104:6–9). In springs and rain they rejoiced in God's provision (104:10–18). In the cycle of day and night they felt God's rhythm (104:19–23). Throughout the creation they understood the Creator's wisdom (104:24). In the playfulness of fish they marveled at God's creativity (104:25–26). In the bounty of the creation they rejoiced in the bounty of God (104:27–30).

The ancients did not have their heads in the sand. They knew there was trouble in the world (104:32, 35a). But they were not myopic. They had the eyes to see a wonderful world all around them and the hearts to feel great joy in this wonderful world. From the distant past this ancient poem invites us to see what they saw, to feel what they felt. Psalm 104 invites us to see the Creator in all that he has made and to be filled with joy in this wonderful world.

The Praise of God's Glory (Psalm 104:33, 35b)

I will sing to the LORD as long as I live.
I will praise my God to my last breath! . . .
As for me—I will praise the LORD!
Praise the LORD!

In addition to great joy, this wonderful world that God has made calls forth great praise from us. The praise of God's majesty, wisdom, bounty, and glory is a fitting conclusion to Psalm 104.

Underneath the two verbs ("to sing" and "to praise") used in 104:33–35 of the NLT are four different Hebrew words. These four words build a staircase on which we can ascend to the heights of the praise of God. The first word is well translated by the English word *sing*. From this word we learn that praise breaks the bounds of ordinary speech. In response to the wonderful world that God has made we are moved not simply to speak God's praise but to sing it out. Singing obviously engages the body, and it engages the whole inner person: the mind, the spirit, and the emotions. "All that is within me, *bless* His holy name," says the psalmist in 103:1 (NASB). The whole person responds to God when we praise him with singing.

The second word is often translated "to sing praise" but is better translated "to make music." Whereas the first word refers to the vocal dimension of song, this sec-

45

ond word adds the idea of using instruments. The instruments used are not always specified but sometimes they are. They include the ten-stringed harp (33:2), the lyre (71:22), and the tambourine (149:3). While the human praise of God is always verbal, it is more than verbal. As 150:3–4 commands:

> Praise him with a blast of the *trumpet*;
>   praise him with the *lyre* and *harp*!
> Praise him with the *tambourine* and dancing;
>   praise him with *stringed instruments* and *flutes*!

The use of instruments adds to the grandeur of the praise given to the God who has fashioned this grand creation.

These first two verbs occur in a special form at the end of Psalm 104. This special form, called a cohortative, is used here to express a firm resolve on the part of the poet.[13] Because God has made such a wonderful world, we commit ourselves to singing his praises.

The third word is traditionally translated "to bless" (NASB). When God is the subject of this verb and we are the object, "to bless" means "to empower for abundant life."[14] When we are the subject and God is the object, "to bless" means "to praise God for empowering us to live an abundant life."[15] At the end of Psalm 104 "to bless" means "to praise God for his majesty, wisdom, bounty, and glory that we are empowered to experience in this wonderful world that he has made."

The underlying Hebrew is identical to the opening words of the psalm. Psalm 104 opens and closes on the same note: "Praise the LORD, I tell myself." The verb used here is an imperative. With this imperative the psalmist exhorts himself and invites us to confess that God is the ultimate source of abundant life in this wonderful world.

The final word is the customary word for "praise." This word means to acknowledge and confess who God is and what he has done on our behalf, and in so doing to give him honor.[16] While the form of the verb is an imperative, the function is that of an exclamation.[17] A transliteration of the Hebrew is the origin of our exclamation, "Hallelujah!" An ecstatic exclamation of praise erupts from the psalmist's lips as the final response to God's wonderful world: "Praise the LORD!"

"Faith comes from listening," says the Apostle Paul in Romans 10:17. If we listen to Psalm 104 we will have the faith to believe that this world in which we live is truly a wonderful world. The fruit of this faith is hearts that are full of joy in and praise for the creation and the Creator. May the maker of heaven and earth grant us the gifts of joy and praise that come from the simply profound exclamation: What a wonderful world!

For Further Reflection
Representative Songs of Praise

Psalms 8, 19, 29, 33, 65, 67, 68, 93, 96, 98, 100, 103, 104, 105, 111, 113, 114, 117, 135, 145, 146, 147, 148, 149, 150

3 O Lord, How Long? The Songs of Lament

O Lord, how long will you forget me? Forever?
   How long will you look the other way?
How long must I struggle with anguish in my soul,
   with sorrow in my heart every day?
   How long will my enemy have the upper hand?

Turn and answer me, O Lord my God!
   Restore the light to my eyes, or I will die.
Don't let my enemies gloat, saying, "We have defeated
      him!"
   Don't let them rejoice at my downfall.

But I trust in your unfailing love.
   I will rejoice because you have rescued me.
I will sing to the Lord
   because he has been so good to me. (Psalm 13)

IN THE SUMMER of 1988 my wife and I packed up our household and moved from Maryland to California. Adele was seven months pregnant at the time, and we were accompanied by our two-year-old and four-year-old sons. For reasons still unknown to us, we left behind not only the East Coast, but also the well-ordered life we had known for thirteen years. The next eleven years were to be characterized by one trouble after another. These years began with an emergency C-section to save the life of our third son and ended with an emergency move back to the East Coast, to Florida, to save our family from hostile opposition.

Most of us have experienced trouble to one degree or another and for longer or shorter stretches of time. The journey of life may take us over very difficult terrain. Adversity replaces prosperity. Turmoil swallows up tranquility. Chaos obliterates order. Doubt replaces faith. Though happy songs can hardly pass from our lips at such times, God has, nevertheless, given us songs to sing even then. These are the songs of lament.

The Book of Psalms contains more songs of lament than any other kind of psalm. About seventy psalms fit into this category. Some of these songs were composed for the community, while others were written for individual use. Though there are differences between the two categories, we will treat the community and individual laments as one genre.

The dominant mood of the songs of lament is dark. Were these psalms being composed in our day and age, they would no doubt be set to blues tunes. Readers immediately feel the pathos of the songs of lament. Feelings of grief, loneliness, perplexity, anger, frustration, abandonment, despair, and more come to expression in the lyrics of these songs. Through the songs of lament the Holy Spirit teaches us, among other lessons, that it is okay to be brutally honest with ourselves and with God when the days are dark and the nights are cold.

While the dominant note is sad in the laments, the final note is usually upbeat. The laments almost always move from negative to positive, from plea to praise. Only two laments do not exhibit this movement: Psalms 44 and 88. Psalm 88 is the darkest song of lament, ending with no hope:

> You have taken my companions and loved ones
>   from me;
>   the darkness is my closest friend. (NIV)

Or, in the language of the NLT:

> You have taken away my companions and loved
>   ones;
>   only darkness remains.

But such despair is the exception in the laments, not the rule. Movement from plea to praise is expected in the laments.[1]

Laments typically answer three questions associated with the plea. The first question is "who?" "Who will hear the psalmist pray?" Language like "O God" and "O Lord" regularly punctuates the beginning of laments:

> O Lord, I have so many enemies. (3:1)

> Answer me when I call, O God. (4:1)

> O Lord, hear me as I pray. (5:1)

51

> O Lord, do not rebuke me. (6:1)

> Keep me safe, O God. (16:1)

"God" translates the Hebrew word *elohim* and refers to God as transcendent, as far above us, as the God of the universe. In keeping with this, "God" is the way the Creator is referred to in Genesis 1, where we read of God's creation of the universe. "Lord," on the other hand, is the English rendering of God's personal name,[2] the name by which God relates intimately with people. "Lord" is, appropriately, the way the Creator is referred to in Genesis 2, where we read of God's personal relationship with humans in the garden of Eden. The point is that the Psalms teach us to call out to the one who is at the same time the Almighty God of the universe and the ever-so-close and personal Lord. Psalm 109:26 captures both of these perspectives with these words: "Help me, *O Lord my God!*"

A second question the psalmist's plea answers is "why?" "Why am I experiencing trouble?" Here we discover the nature of the trouble that the psalmist is in and the reason(s) for the lament. The words *complaint* and *confession* provide pegs on which we can hang the thoughts of the psalmist's answer to the "why?"

The complaint is not a rebellious complaining like that of Israel in the wilderness (e.g., Numbers 11:1; 14:2; 16:11). The complaint is simply the psalmist spelling out with great emotion the struggles being experienced. This complaint can go in three directions. In the Psalms, the complaint may be directed toward the self, toward other people, or toward God:

O LORD, hear me as I pray;
    pay attention to *my groaning*. (5:1)

O LORD, I have *so many enemies*. (3:1)

LORD, why do *you* stand so far away? (10:1)

Honesty is the operative word here. Through the laments the Holy Spirit gives us great encouragement and great freedom to bring to expression *all* that we are thinking and feeling, whether those thoughts and feelings are about ourselves, others, or even God himself. As we will discover in our study of Psalm 13, stuffing our thoughts and emotions does not help at all, and expressing how we feel and what we think is part of the path to renewal.

The confession may go in one of two directions. Often the psalmist confesses his sin. Psalm 38:3–5 contains a good example:

Because of your anger, my whole body is sick;
    my health is broken because of my sins.
My guilt overwhelms me—
    it is a burden too heavy to bear.
My wounds fester and stink
    because of my foolish sins.

There is often a connection in life between character and consequence. Living in keeping with God's instruction enhances life,[3] while violating divine principles diminishes life. When reading the laments, therefore, we often hear a confession of sin in the context of the experience of trouble.[4]

53

On the other hand, the confession may be of the psalmist's innocence. Psalm 26:1–3 provides one of the best examples of such a confession:

> Declare me innocent, O Lord,
>   for I have acted with integrity;
>   I have trusted in the Lord without wavering.
> Put me on trial, Lord, and cross-examine me.
>   Test my motives and affections.
> For I am constantly aware of your unfailing love,
>   and I have lived according to your truth.

This is not the prayer of a misguided and self-righteous person, because the David who in Psalm 26 confesses his innocence is the same David who has just confessed his sin in Psalm 25:

> Forgive the rebellious sins of my youth. (25:7)

> O Lord, forgive my many, many sins. (25:11)

> Forgive all my sins. (25:18)

Psalm 26 is the prayer that David offered in a particular situation in which he was accused of some wrongdoing, but was in fact innocent. David experienced the pain of false accusations many times in his life, and when he did, his lamentation included a confession of his innocence (e.g., 4:1–2; 7:1–8). Through the laments the Holy Spirit teaches us to confess our sin, when appropriate, and to say, "I am innocent," when we are in the right.

The third question the plea seeks to answer is "what?" "What does the psalmist want God to do?" Concreteness characterizes the psalmist's pleas at this point in the lament. The psalmist makes very specific requests of God, requests that correspond to the nature of the trouble. Has the psalmist sinned? The request is for forgiveness:

> *Forgive* the rebellious sins of my youth;
>> look instead through the eyes of your unfailing
>>> love,
>> for you are merciful, O LORD. (25:7)

> Help us, O God of our salvation!
>> Help us for the honor of your name.
> Oh, save us and *forgive* our sins
>> for the sake of your name. (79:9)

Is the psalmist ill? The request is for healing:

> Have compassion on me, LORD, for I am weak.
>> *Heal* me, LORD, for my body is in agony. (6:2)

> "O LORD," I prayed, "have mercy on me.
>> *Heal* me, for I have sinned against you." (41:4)

Has the psalmist been falsely accused? The request is for vindication:

> *Declare me innocent*, O LORD, for I have acted with
>> integrity;
> I have trusted in the LORD without wavering.
>> (26:1)

> O God, take up my cause!
>> *Defend* me against these ungodly people.
>> Rescue me from these unjust liars. (43:1)

Is the psalmist under attack by adversaries? The request is for deliverance:

> Arise, O LORD!
>> Stand against them and bring them to their
>>> knees!
>> *Rescue* me from the wicked with your sword!
>>> (17:13)

> My future is in your hands.
>> *Rescue* me from those who hunt me down relent-
>>> lessly. (31:15)

Is the psalmist weak? The request is for support:

> LORD, *sustain* me as you promised, that I may live!
>> Do not let my hope be crushed.
> *Sustain* me, and I will be saved;
>> then I will meditate on your principles continu-
>>> ally. (119:116–17)

In all of these requests the psalmists are very much concerned with experiencing the help of God in this life. This is not to say that the Psalms have no interest in the life to come. It is to say that through the Psalms the Holy Spirit teaches us that we can expect God's salvation to affect our lives now in concrete ways. This confident expectation comes to expression perhaps nowhere more clearly than in 27:13:

> Yet I am confident that I will see the LORD's
>> goodness
> while I am here in the land of the living.

The plea is usually the larger of the two sections of a lament. The praise section is characteristically shorter and is positive in tone. The praise section may contain, for example, a statement of trust or confidence:

> I will lie down in peace and sleep,
> for you alone, O Lord, will keep me safe. (4:8)

> On the very day I call to you for help,
> my enemies will retreat.
> This I know: God is on my side. (56:9)

The psalmist may also express a deep assurance that God will answer prayer and grant the request made in the plea section:

> The Lord has heard my plea;
> the Lord will answer my prayer. (6:9)

> Lord, you know the hopes of the helpless.
> Surely you will listen to their cries and comfort
> them. (10:17)

The praise section may also contain a vow or promise to give God thanks and offer sacrifice at the temple after God answers the psalmist's prayer. Psalm 66:13–14 refers to the making of such a vow:

> Now I come to your Temple with burnt offerings
> to fulfill the vows I made to you—
> yes, the sacred vows you heard me make
> when I was in deep trouble.

Laments record such vows:

57

I will praise you among all the people;
 I will fulfill my vows in the presence of those
  who worship you. (22:25)

I will fulfill my vows to you, O God,
 and offer a sacrifice of thanks for your help.
 (56:12)

Having studied the lament in general terms, let's now turn to Psalm 13 to study a particular lament. Psalm 13 contains most of the typical elements of a lament and brings to expression the thoughts and feeling of a person in deep distress. For these reasons Psalm 13 provides a wonderful example of the lament and offers marvelous insights into how to process our thoughts and emotions in times of trouble.

I have outlined Psalm 13 according to the three natural divisions in the Psalms. Psalm 13:1–2 is dominated by the repeated question, "How long, O Lord?" Here the psalmist expresses his feelings. Psalm 13:3–4 is a series of requests, expressing what the psalmist wants God to do. Psalm 13:5–6 is affirmations of the psalmist's confidence that God will intervene and the psalmist's resolve to rejoice as he waits for God to act. By means of this threefold division the Holy Spirit teaches you to say how you feel, to ask for what you want, and to trust God for the results.

Say How You Feel (Psalm 13:1–2)

Sometimes an hour can feel like an eternity, especially if you have to wait for someone in a time of deep distress. Have you ever felt as if you were waiting forever for God to act on you behalf? That is exactly how David must have felt when he said, "O LORD, how long will you forget me? *Forever?*"

Getting in Touch with Your Feelings

You have feelings. To be human is to feel. You are more than feelings, but without feelings you are less than fully human. This is true because you have been created in the image of God (Genesis 1:26–27) and God feels.

God feels affection and love:

> Yet the LORD set his *affection* on your forefathers and *loved* them, and he chose you, their descendants, above all the nations, as it is today. (Deuteronomy 10:15 NIV)

God feels joy and happiness:

> For the LORD your God has arrived to live among you. He is a mighty savior. He will *rejoice* over you with great *gladness*. With his love, he will calm all your fears. He will *exult* over you by singing a *happy* song. (Zephaniah 3:17)

God feels jealousy:

> Do not worship any other god, for the LORD, whose name is *Jealous*, is a *jealous* God. (Exodus 34:14 NIV)

God feels grief and pain:

> The LORD was *grieved* that he had made man on the earth, and his heart was filled with *pain*. (Genesis 6:6 NIV)

God feels anger:

> Then the Lord became *angry* with Moses. (Exodus
> 4:14)

Since God feels and since you are created in God's image, feelings are part of your human experience.

How did David feel, when he wrote the words of Psalm 13:1–2? David felt abandoned when he said:

> O Lord, how long will you forget me? Forever?
> How long will you look the other way?

David also felt deep sorrow:

> How long must I struggle with anguish in my soul,
> with sorrow in my heart every day?

David felt frustrated:

> How long will my enemy have the upper hand?

And David felt weary, as is clear from his references to being sad "every day" and "forever."

David's feelings are common human feelings. I've had these same feelings, and you no doubt have as well. Haven't you felt at times as if God had abandoned you? Haven't you felt a deep sadness that you thought would never end? Haven't you felt frustrated when reaching your goal seemed impossible? Haven't you felt weary of it all when hours turned into days and days turned into weeks? That's okay. Such feelings are part of the human experience.

Your feelings go in three directions. You have three relationships in life: relationships with God, with other people, and with yourself. That is why Jesus said, "You must love the Lord your God" and "love your neighbor as yourself" (Matthew 22:37–39). Since you have these three relationships, it is not surprising that you have feelings that go in three directions: feelings toward God, toward others, and toward yourself. All three are found in Psalm 13:1–2. David felt abandoned by God, sadness and weariness within his own soul, and frustration with his adversaries who had the upper hand.

Perhaps you or someone close to you is like me. I am not always in touch with how I feel. Sometimes my wife knows how I feel before I do. I sometimes come home, and Adele will say, "What's the matter?" To which I reply, "Nothing." After time and talking Adele draws out the feelings inside me that I was not in touch with. The Holy Spirit has given you the Book of Psalms for many reasons, one of which is to help you get in touch with how you feel. This is why John Calvin said:

> I have been accustomed to calling the Book of Psalms an Anatomy of All the Parts of the Soul. For there is not an emotion of which anyone can be conscious that is not here represented as in a mirror. Rather the Holy Spirit has here drawn to the life all the griefs, sorrows, fears, doubts, hopes, cares, perplexities with which the minds of men are want to be agitated.[5]

Calvin compares the Psalms to a mirror. When you read the Psalms you see a reflection of all the emotions that you feel from time to time in life. Reading the Psalms is like talking to my wife: the Psalms help me get in touch with how I feel about God, others, and myself. They can do the same for you.

The Psalms give you freedom to feel. And they teach you what to do with your feelings.

Expressing Your Feelings in Words

Stuffing your feelings does not help. Sometimes we live in denial of how we feel or we bottle up how we feel, thinking this is the best or most spiritual way to handle our feelings. David once said:

> I will watch my ways
> and keep my tongue from sin;
> I will put a muzzle on my mouth
> as long as the wicked are in my presence.
> (39:1 NIV)

But rather than helping, this only made matters worse for David:

> But when I was silent and still,
> not even saying anything good,
> my anguish increased.
> My heart grew hot within me,
> and as I meditated, the fire burned. (39:2–3 NIV)

You've probably been in David's shoes before. You determined not to say anything, but the longer you held your feelings in the more intense they grew until you thought you were about to burst. Blurting out every thought and feeling is not what the Bible recommends (Proverbs 10:19; 21:23). The Psalms do teach us, however, that there are times when holding in feelings does not solve the problem but adds to it. As you grow in wisdom you grow in your ability to know when to be silent and when to speak (Ecclesiastes 8:5–6).

Expressing your feelings is beneficial. "Then I spoke with my tongue," said David (Psalm 39:3 NIV). David finally broke his silence and brought to expression what was inside.

I remember when I was a child how my mother would cook spaghetti sauce in a pressure cooker. I can still hear the rattle of the pressure release valve jiggling on top of the cooker. Without that pressure release valve the cooker would have exploded, causing untold damage in the kitchen. Expressing your feelings is like that pressure release valve.

Expressing your feelings is beneficial. Just saying, "O LORD, how long?" helps. As in Psalm 13 and other psalms, David expresses many feelings. He feels worthless, despised, and insulted (22:6–7). He feels foolish, humiliated, and weak (38:5–8). He feels overwhelmed, isolated, and hopeless (88:7–8, 18). All these feelings come to expression in the Psalms. And it is beneficial to bring these kinds of feelings to expression when they are churning within us.

While saying how you feel is an important step to take, it is only the first step, and it leads naturally to the second: Ask for what you want.

Ask For What You Want (Psalm 13:3–4)

"The reason you don't have what you want is that you don't ask" (James 4:2). While some folks may hesitate to ask for what they want, the ancient psalmists did not. As we have already seen, the laments are full of people

asking for things. Psalm 13 is no exception. As with feelings, however, so with desires. Before you can ask for
what you want you have to get in touch with your
desires.

Getting in Touch with Your Desires

> The Lord is my shepherd;
> I shall not *want*. (23:1 KJV)

How many folks have misunderstood this well-known
verse to teach that Christians are not to *want* anything!
The message we have too often received is that to want
things is bad. How ironic that this famous verse says
just about the opposite! It teaches that because the Lord
is our shepherd, we will not *lack* anything![6]

And then there is 73:25:

> Whom have I in heaven *but You*?
> And besides You, *I desire nothing* on earth.
> (NASB)

This verse seems to make it pretty clear that the spiri-
tually mature have no desires except for God. Unless of
course this is an example of hyperbole and intends to
say nothing more than that God is our primary desire.
This is the sense according to the NLT:

> Whom have I in heaven but you?
> I desire you more than anything on earth.

In support of this consider the prayer for the king in
20:4: "May [God] grant your heart's desire"; and consider the thanksgiving in regard to the king in 21:2: "For

you have given him his heart's desire." Another psalm gives you a command and a promise:

> Take delight in the LORD,
> and he will give you *your heart's desires*. (37:4)

If you delight in the Lord, then the Lord will give you what you desire. If the Lord is willing to give you what you desire, then having desires must be okay with the Lord.

What are "your heart's desires"? This is the question. And one of the best ways to get in touch with your desires is to get in touch with your feelings. In other words, the first and second sections of Psalm 13 are related. Getting in touch with how you feel and expressing those feelings leads to getting in touch with what you desire. As getting in touch with your feelings leads to expressing those feeling in words, so getting in touch with your desires leads to asking God specifically for what you want.

Asking God Specifically

"The reason you don't have what you want is that *you don't ask God*" (James 4:2). Prayer is more than asking God to do things for us and give things to us. But prayer includes asking. Jesus taught us to pray/ask, "Give us our food for today" (Matthew 6:11). In Psalm 13 David asks for three specific things: attention, vitality, and success.

David has already expressed that he felt as if God were not paying attention to him, so he now says, "Turn and answer me."[7] David wants God's attention. And David is not content with asking, he wants an answer, and that in the affirmative. There may be times when you feel as

65

if God is just not paying attention. That's okay. Plenty of others have felt this same way. Ask God to pay attention to you and to your situation. Tell God that you no longer want his silence, but that you want him to answer your prayer with his presence. You want that sense in your soul that God's presence is with you, and you want evidence of that presence in your life.

David felt sad and weary, so he now asks God for renewed strength: "Restore the light to my eyes, or I will die." This is not a request for mental illumination but for physical and emotional rejuvenation. Once when Jonathan was exhausted from chasing his enemies, he dipped his staff in wild honey along the road and ate some. The text tells us that "his eyes brightened" (1 Samuel 14:27 NIV). The Hebrew verb is the same one used in Psalm 13:3. Jonathan did not have some kind of miraculous glow from a mystical experience. His face simply gave evidence of renewed energy that came from the sugar in the honey. Distress can zap your energy level, especially when the distress is prolonged. Ask God for the physical and emotional energy you need to make it through to the other side. And do not hesitate to ask passionately. David was in all likelihood not about to die. He used death as a hyperbolic image to make his point with greater passion. You have the freedom to do the same.

The reason that David felt frustrated was that God had promised him success over his enemies:

> Only ask, and I will give you the nations as your inheritance,
>   the ends of the earth as your possession. (2:8)

But David was not experiencing that success. Lack of success is always frustrating, especially in light of God's promise of success to you:

> Whatever they do succeeds. (1:3, my translation)[8]

Praying for success is as biblical as praying for anything else in keeping with God's word. David not only prayed for success for himself here, but elsewhere he prayed for success for others, for example, for Solomon:

> Now, my son, may the LORD be with you and give you success as you follow his instructions in building the Temple of the LORD your God. (1 Chronicles 22:11)

And God answered this prayer and gave Solomon success:

> So Solomon finished building the Temple of the LORD, as well as the royal palace. He completed everything he had planned to do. (2 Chronicles 7:11)

Ask God for success in every area of your life. And expect God to answer your prayer and grant that success.

Attention, vitality, success—while not an exhaustive list of things to ask God for, this certainly is a basic list. For every endeavor in life you need God's attention, God's vitality, and God's success. "Keep on asking, and you will be given what you ask for" (Matthew 7:7).

So far Psalm 13 has taught us two steps for dealing with dark days: say how you feel and ask for what you want. Before we study the final step, let me tell you a story about Bobby.

Bobby and I were great friends growing up. Imagine us as twelve-year-old boys playing little league baseball. Our dream was the same as every twelve-year-old: to play in the all-stars. We both made the team! One highlight for us was playing in Ellwood City, because the field at Ellwood City had lights. Twelve-year-olds playing under the lights! Didn't get any better than that!

Our team made it to the championship game. It was the last inning of the last game. We were ahead with two outs but the opposing team's winning run was on base. Only one out left to win the big trophy and to leave the small trophy for others. I was playing second base, and Bobby was in right field. Bobby was a great ball player.

There are three fundamentals for catching a fly ball: keep your eye on the ball, get under the ball, and squeeze the mitt. Bobby knew these fundamentals well and had executed them successfully many, many times.

The pitch was thrown and there was a high, high fly to right field. Bobby kept his eye on the ball, got right under the ball, and the ball came right into his glove. Victory was ours! But Bobby didn't squeeze the mitt. The ball dropped out and we lost. I'll never forget how sad Bobby felt after not squeezing the mitt.

As important as saying how you feel and asking for what you want are, they don't give you victory if you don't squeeze the mitt. You must take the third step. You must squeeze the mitt. You must trust God for the results.

Trust God for the Results (Psalm 13:5–6)

Note the first words of the final section of Psalm 13: "But I trust." To trust is to have confidence in. To trust is to feel secure with. To trust is to rely on. To trust God for the results is to be confident that God is at work in everything for your good (Romans 8:28), to feel secure with God's purpose for you, to rely on God to work things out in just the right way. Trusting involves exercising your faith by relying on God's character.

Exercising Your Faith

Faith involves personal choice. A wooden translation of the beginning of 13:5 would read, "But I—in your unfailing love I trust." There is an extra "I" put right at the beginning of this sentence in Hebrew, an "I" that is not really needed. By including this extra "I" the psalmist focuses attention on himself. There is a "strong emotional heightening" and "focused attention or deep self-consciousness" expressed by this additional "I."[9]

The point is that the mitt does not squeeze itself and no one can squeeze the mitt for you. To squeeze or not to squeeze is your choice. Having said how you feel and having asked for what you want, squeeze the mitt—choose for yourself to rely on God to work things out in just the right way. Choose to trust that God is at work in your present circumstances and that he will work out everything for your good. That is faith: believing before seeing. And faith is your personal choice in every situation.

Faith produces firm resolve. The Hebrew verbs translated "I will rejoice" and "I will sing" are not declarative verbs; they are not the verbs ordinarily used to make simple statements. These two verbs are volitives; they are special verbs used to express the strong will of the

69

speaker in any number of ways. In 13:5 these verbs are used to express firm resolve.[10]

David firmly resolves to rejoice in the Lord and to sing to the Lord. This firm resolve was possible because David had first chosen to trust that the Lord would work things out in the way that was the very best for David. By faith you, too, can resolve to rejoice in God's reversal of your circumstances before you see that reversal in reality. Believe it before you see it, and you, too, can sing for joy in anticipation of receiving it.

The crucial question at this point is, "Where do you get such faith?" How is it possible for you to believe it before you see it? You find the answer in the character of God.

Relying on God's Character

All of God's characteristics make God trustworthy. At this point, however, the psalmist does not choose to list all of God's character traits. Rather, David focuses our attention on two: God's unfailing love and God's generosity.

God's unfailing love. There is a proverb that says, "What a man desires is unfailing love" (Proverbs 19:22 NIV).[11] A profound human desire—perhaps the most profound human desire—is to be loved unconditionally, to be loved in spite of what we do rather than because of what we do, to be loved with a love that will never fail. That is the sense of the Hebrew word translated "unfailing love." When used of God, this word refers to God's utter loyalty to you, his utter faithfulness to you, his love that will never ever fail you.

You can trust God because he is characterized by unfailing love for you, by a love that will not let you go, by a love that can only do what is the very best for you. In the darkest of days you can say by faith:

> Yet I still dare to hope when I remember this:
> The unfailing love of the LORD never ends!
> (Lamentations 3:21–22)

Nothing can ever stop this love that God has for you. No trouble or calamity, no hunger or cold, no angels or demons, no fears for today or worries about tomorrow, not even threats of death or the powers of hell can stop this love that God has for you (Romans 8:35–38). This love that is God's very character is why you can trust God to work out everything for your good (8:28).

The proof that God has this love for you is seen in his gift of Christ to you. God gave you his Son to live a perfect life in your place, to die on the cross to pay for your sins, and to be raised from the dead to empower you for new life, so it is utterly unthinkable that God would now fail to give you everything else you need (Romans 8:32). You can rely on God's unfailing love.

God's generosity. The final words of Psalm 13 are, "Because he has dealt bountifully with me" (ESV, NASB, NKJV, NRSV). The psalm ends by focusing your attention on God's bountiful, generous character. You can trust God to work things out in the very best way for you, because God is a generous God.

While translations regularly use a past tense in this final clause ("has dealt"), I think a future tense is more appropriate ("will deal") for two reasons. First, though

71

the Hebrew verb is a past tense, this type of verb can be used for a situation in the future that is so certain that one can speak of it as already accomplished in the past.[12] This use of the past for the future expresses the certainty of the future situation with much more power. Second, this same verb is used again in the Psalms at the end of a similar psalm, and the verb form used is the one typically used for the future: "For You will deal bountifully with me" (142:7 NASB). The psalmist could trust God to do the best, because the psalmist could rely on God to be generous with him in the future. So can you.

God says to you:

> It was I, the LORD your God,
>   who rescued you from the land of Egypt.
>   Open your mouth wide, and I will fill it with
>   good things. . . .
> I would feed you with the best of foods.
>   I would satisfy you with wild honey from the
>   rock. (81:10, 16)

These are the words of an extremely generous God who loves to give good gifts to his children.

Jesus has told you to be like your Father (Luke 6:36), to forgive like your Father forgives (6:37), and to give like your Father gives (6:38). And how does your Father give? *"A good measure, pressed down, shaken together and running over, will be poured into your lap"* (6:38 NIV). That is how your generous Father gives. That is what your generous God is like. That is why you can trust God to work things out for you in the best possible way!

May your journey through life never take you down a dark path. But if it does, remember the simple lessons from Psalm 13. Say how you feel. Ask for what you want. Trust God for the results. You can. He has already given you his Son. He will now give you everything else you need (Romans 8:32)!

For Further Reflection
Representative Songs of Lament

Psalms 3, 5, 6, 7, 13, 17, 22, 25, 26, 27, 28, 38, 39, 42, 43, 44, 51, 54, 55, 56, 57, 59, 61, 63, 64, 69, 70, 71, 74, 79, 80, 83, 86, 88, 89, 102, 109, 120, 130, 140, 141, 142, 143

MOURNING TO DANCING! THE SONGS OF THANKSGIVING

A psalm of David, sung at the dedication of the Temple.

I will praise you, LORD, for you have rescued me.
*   You refused to let my enemies triumph over me.*
O LORD my God, I cried out to you for help,
*   and you restored my health.*
You brought me up from the grave, O LORD.
*   You kept me from falling into the pit of death.*

Sing to the LORD, all you godly ones!
*   Praise his holy name.*
His anger lasts for a moment,
*   but his favor lasts a lifetime!*
Weeping may go on all night,
*   but joy comes with the morning.*

75

When I was prosperous I said,
  "Nothing can stop me now!"
Your favor, O LORD, made me as secure as a mountain.
  Then you turned away from me, and I was shattered.

I cried out to you, O LORD.
  I begged the LORD for mercy, saying,
"What will you gain if I die,
  if I sink down into the grave?
Can my dust praise you from the grave?
  Can it tell the world of your faithfulness?
Hear me, LORD, and have mercy on me.
  Help me, O LORD."

You have turned my mourning into joyful dancing.
  You have taken away my clothes of mourning and
    clothed me with joy,
that I might sing praises to you and not be silent.
  O LORD my God, I will give you thanks forever!
  (Psalm 30)

IN THE SUMMER of 1999 my wife and I packed up our household once again and moved this time from California to Florida. In place of California's one-crisis-after-another experience, Florida has been and is a place of green pastures and still waters for us as a family. God has reversed our circumstances and replaced turmoil with rest—through the community at Reformed Theological Seminary, my denominational leaders, local churches we have attended, our family's involvement in the Seminole County Public Schools (where the children attend and my wife works as a guidance counselor), and wonderful friends we have made. The words of Psalm 40:2 ring true in our ears:

> He lifted me out of the pit of despair,
> out of the mud and the mire.
> He set my feet on solid ground
> and steadied me as I walked along.

It is for times such as these that the ancient psalmists composed the songs of thanksgiving.

In one word, thanksgiving is the basic content of these songs. The songs of thanksgiving are like the songs of praise in that the overall mood and overarching theme are positive. The primary difference is focus. The songs of praise tend to focus on the distant past, when, for example, God created the universe or delivered the psalmist's ancestors at the time of the exodus from Egypt. The songs of thanksgiving, on the other hand, focus on the immediate past, when, for example, God healed the psalmist from sickness or delivered him from hostile foes.

The Hebrew verb translated "give thanks" is *hodah*. Hebrew *hodah* means "to acknowledge" or "to confess."[1] This verb is used for acknowledging or confessing one's sins:

> I said to myself, "I will confess [*hodah*] my rebellion to the LORD."
> And you forgave me! All my guilt is gone. (32:5)

But most of the time *hodah* is used for acknowledging or confessing the good things that God has done for the psalmist. Since "praising" is acknowledging or confessing who God is and what God has done (see chap-

77

ter 2, pages 24–25), "giving thanks" and "praising" are closely related. This is why the verb *hodah* is at times translated "to praise." For example, the NLT of 18:49 says:

> For this, O Lord, I will praise [*hodah*] you among
> the nations;
> I will sing joyfully to your name.

In general, to give thanks is to praise God. In particular, to give thanks is to praise God for answered prayer, and the prayer answered is that recorded in the song of lament.[2] Simply put, the song of thanksgiving is the sequel to the song of lament. In 54:2–3 David laments:

> O God, listen to my prayer.
> Pay attention to my plea.
> For strangers are attacking me;
> violent men are trying to kill me.
> They care nothing for God.

Then in 54:6 David makes this vow:

> I will sacrifice a voluntary offering to you;
> I will praise [*hodah*] your name, O Lord,
> for it is good.

When in distress an ancient believer would vow to do any number of things if God would just deliver. Two things frequently vowed were the giving of thanks and the offering of sacrifice, and as we will now see, these two were closely related in ancient Israel.

The Hebrew noun *todah* is related to the verb *hodah*. The noun *todah* is used to refer to two separate but related things: (1) a *song* of thanksgiving and (2) a *sacrifice* of thanksgiving.[3] Hebrew *todah* is used for a *song* of thanksgiving in many psalms:

> Then I will praise God's name with singing,
>> and I will honor him with thanksgiving [*todah*].
>> (69:30)

> Sing out your thanks [*todah*] to the LORD;
>> sing praises to our God, accompanied by harps.
>> (147:7)

The song of thanksgiving was a means by which ancient Israelites publicly acknowledged what God had done for them in delivering them from this or that trouble. At the temple the grateful worshiper would invite other worshipers to gather around and to listen to the recital of the good things God had just done. One such invitation is found in 66:13–14, 16:

> Now I come to your Temple with burnt offerings
>> to fulfill the vows I made to you—
> yes, the sacred vows you heard me make
>> when I was in deep trouble. . . .
> Come and listen, all you who fear God,
>> and I will tell you what he did for me.

When in trouble the psalmist promised to tell others of God's goodness, once deliverance had been experienced. Having been delivered, the psalmist fulfills his vow by using a song of thanksgiving to tell others what God had done.

Ancient worship included the opportunity for God's people to share publicly their experiences on life's journey. The song of thanksgiving gave them opportunity to share their sorrows and their joys, their defeats and their victories, their doubts and their faith, their selves and their God. Contemporary worship is all the richer when we follow the ancient example. Not only clerics but also lay believers can encourage the community and glorify God through public thanksgiving. Public thanksgiving is one valuable way for the congregation to participate in the public worship of God.

Hebrew *todah* is also used for a *sacrifice* of thanksgiving in Psalms like 56:12–13:

> I will fulfill my vows to you, O God,
> > and offer a sacrifice of thanks [*todah*] for your
> > help.
> For you have rescued me from death;
> > you have kept my feet from slipping.

The use of *todah* in reference to a sacrifice of thanksgiving explains why in the middle of Psalm 66 (cited above) we read in 66:15:

> That is why I am sacrificing burnt offerings to you—
> > the best of my rams as a pleasing aroma.
> And I will sacrifice bulls and goats.

The sacrifice of thanksgiving was one of the sacrifices of which the worshipers would have eaten a portion. Leviticus 7:13–15 refers to this sacrificial meal this way:

> This peace offering of thanksgiving [*todah*] must also be accompanied by loaves of yeast bread. One of each kind of bread must be presented as a gift to the LORD. This bread will then belong to the priest who

sprinkles the altar with blood from the sacrificed animal. The animal's meat must be eaten on the same day it is offered. None of it may be saved for the next morning.

That the sacrifice of thanksgiving was a festive meal explains texts like Psalm 22:25–26:

> I will praise you among all the people;
>> I will fulfill my vows in the presence of those
>>> who worship you.
> The poor will eat and be satisfied.
>> All who seek the LORD will praise him.
>> Their hearts will rejoice with everlasting joy.

The poor eating in the context of a vow being paid makes perfect sense, since part of the payment was the offering of a sacrifice of thanksgiving. And a wealthy person would have offered rams, bulls, and goats (66:15) upon which many who rarely had the luxury of eating meat could feast to their hearts' content. The song of thanksgiving thus functioned as one key component of grateful worship that celebrated the goodness of God in delivering people from trouble in this life.

That the song of thanksgiving is the sequel to the song of lament is clear from its basic content, and it is equally clear from part of its basic structure. Songs of thanksgiving can often be divided into three sections. The opening section typically opens with the psalmist's intention to praise or thank God:

> I will praise the LORD at all times.
>> I will constantly speak his praises. (34:1)

81

> We thank you, O God!
>   We give thanks because you are near.
>   People everywhere tell of your mighty miracles.
>   (75:1)

The song of thanksgiving may also begin on a note of loving gratitude for divine intervention:

> I love the LORD because he hears
>   and answers my prayers. (116:1)

> I love you, LORD; you are my strength. (18:1)

The central section mirrors the song of lament, as the psalmist here recounts his trouble, petition, and deliverance. Sometimes this recounting is fairly extensive. In Psalm 18 David recounts his past experience twice (18:4–19, 31–45). At other times the recounting of the past is much briefer:

> I prayed to the LORD, and he answered me,
>   freeing me from all my fears.
> Those who look to him for help will be radiant with
>   joy;
>   no shadow of shame will darken their faces.
> I cried out to the LORD in my suffering, and he
>   heard me.
> He set me free from all my fears. (34:4–6)

The concluding section is typically characterized by thanksgiving. The thanksgiving may be continued praise and thanks offered by the psalmist:

> Praise God, who did not ignore my prayer

and did not withdraw his unfailing love from
    me. (66:20)

Or the thanksgiving may come in the form of a promise to praise God in the future:

> For this, O Lord, I will praise you among the
>   nations;
> I will sing joyfully to your name. (18:49)

Or the psalmist may conclude by inviting others to join
in the thanksgiving:

> Give thanks to the Lord, for he is good!
>   His faithful love endures forever. (118:29)

Having come to understand the basic content and
structure of the songs of thanksgiving, let's now study
Psalm 30 as a prime example of this genre. The theme
of thanksgiving runs through the entire psalm, and
the Hebrew word *hodah* is repeated three times in
30:4, 9, and 12:

> Sing to the Lord, all you godly ones!
>   Praise [*hodah*] his holy name. . . .
> Can my dust praise [*hodah*] you from the grave?
>   Can it tell the world of your faithfulness? . . .
> O Lord my God, I will give you thanks [*hodah*]
>   forever!

Psalm 30 gives thanks to God for the great reversal of
circumstances the psalmist has experienced in his life
and provides us with a marvelous model to follow.
    Psalm 30 has a historical note in the title:[4]

> A psalm of David, sung at the dedication of the Temple.

Most of the time it is easy to see the connection between the historical note and the content of the psalm. Such is not the case with Psalm 30. As we will see, the psalm is obviously a song of thanksgiving for deliverance from a grave illness. How does that fit with "sung at the dedication of the Temple," since David was not alive when the temple was dedicated? First, the word translated "temple" is the Hebrew word *bayit*. The word *bayit* can refer to an ordinary house (49:16), the house of a king ("palace"; Gen 12:15 NIV), or the house of God, whether that is the temple (Psalm 5:7) or the earlier tabernacle (Judges 18:31). It is quite possible to imagine a situation that could bridge the apparent gap between the title and the content of Psalm 30. For example, it is possible that Psalm 30 was composed for the dedication of David's palace (2 Samuel 5:11–12; 7:1) or the dedication of the special tent David had constructed to house the ark of the covenant (6:17), with either dedication having been delayed owing to an illness David had. While the meaning of the note in the title is a bit obscure, the meaning of the psalm is not.

Psalm 30 actually contains two songs of thanksgiving, as it were. In 30:1–5 the psalmist expresses his intention to give thanks and tells his story in brief in 30:1–3, and he then invites the community to celebrate God's reversal of his circumstances in 30:4–5. In 30:6–12 the psalmist covers much the same terrain only in greater detail, telling his story of trouble in 30:6–10 and celebrating God's reversal of his circumstances in 30:11–12. So we will analyze the psalm according to a fourfold division: summarizing the experience (30:1–3), including the community (30:4–5), recounting the details (30:6–10), and celebrating the reversal (30:11–12).

Summarizing the Experience (Psalm 30:1–3)

The first part of 30:1 really tells the whole story in the briefest form: the psalmist intends to praise the Lord because the Lord rescued him. As of yet, we do not know from what the psalmist was rescued but there is a hint in the Hebrew that underlies the English "rescued."

Rescued from the Well

The Hebrew word translated "rescued" is *dalah* and is used only a few times in the Old Testament. Several times it is used with a literal sense of "to draw up"; in Exodus 2:16, 19 *dalah* is used for drawing water up out of a well. This verb is used figuratively in Proverbs 20:5, where the human heart is like a well filled with rich resources that a wise person can "draw out." A figurative sense is also at play in Psalm 30:1. God's rescue was a "drawing up" of some kind. Like water is drawn up out of a well, the Lord drew the psalmist up out of trouble.

Rescued from the Grave

Psalm 30:3 makes clear just what this "well" was. It was the "grave" or the "pit of death." The psalmist was in the grave or the pit of death, as it were, and the Lord graciously drew him up out of there.

When the psalmist says, "You brought me up from the grave, O LORD," we should not understand this as a resurrection experience, for several reasons. First, the following part of the verse says, "You kept me from falling into the pit of death." The Hebrew verb here means to keep alive or preserve alive.[5] God did not let the psalmist actually die. Second, the previous verse says, "I cried out to you for help, and you restored my health." Dead people do not cry out to God, and "restored my health" means "healed me." So why did the psalmist say, "You brought me up from the grave, O LORD"? This is a graphic way of portraying how ill the psalmist was. In modern terms he "had one foot in the grave" or "was on the verge of death." David had been *gravely* ill and the Lord had rescued him, had drawn him up and out of that *grave* illness like one draws up water from a well. And for this David gives much thanks to God.

The language of Psalm 16:10 is quite similar to that of 30:4:

> For you do not give me up to Sheol,
>   or let your faithful one see the Pit. (NRSV)

The Hebrew word translated "Sheol" in 16:10 is the same word translated "grave" in 30:4, and the word translated "Pit" in 16:10 is a synonym of the word translated "pit" in 30:4. In 16:10 the psalmist is expressing confidence that God will not let him die rather than confidence that God will raise him from the dead. Yet the New Testament quotes 16:10 in reference to Jesus' resurrection from the dead (Acts 13:35). How can this be?

I think the answer lies in the truth that what the psalmists experienced in a limited way Jesus experienced to the ultimate extreme. For example, David said in Psalm 22:1, "My God, my God! Why have you forsaken me?" David certainly felt forsaken, as perhaps you have in some season of your life, but David was not truly forsaken by God. Jesus also prayed these same words on the cross (Matthew 27:46), where he not only felt forsaken but actually was forsaken by the Father, because he was carrying the sins of the world on his shoulders. Jesus experienced all that David experienced *and then some*. So, too, David experienced being rescued from a grave illness, but Jesus experienced being rescued from the grave itself. Jesus experienced all that David experienced *and then some*. No matter what you experience in any season of life, Jesus understands and can sympathize with you (Hebrews 4:15), because Jesus has had your experience *and then some*.

Rescued from the Enemy

One final question before moving to the second section: Why the reference to the enemies in Psalm 30:1 if David was rescued from illness? We cannot answer this question with precision but we can offer at least one valid perspective. Illness and vulnerability go together. When David was ill, he was also vulnerable. David's enemies would have tried to capitalize on his illness in one way or another. Psalm 38 expresses this. In 38:1–10 the psalmist describes a severe illness. Then in 38:11–20 he describes the reaction of friends and foes to his illness. Of interest to us at this point is the reaction of the foes recorded in 30:12, 19–20:

> Meanwhile, my enemies lay traps for me;
> they make plans to ruin me.

> They think up treacherous deeds all day long. . . .
> My enemies are many;
>> they hate me though I have done nothing against
>> them.
> They repay me evil for good
> and oppose me because I stand for the right.

The expression "kick a man when he is down" was unfortunately born in such circumstances.

So the psalmist prayed, "Don't let my enemies gloat over me" (38:16). The verb translated "gloat" is the same word translated "triumph" in 30:1. The word means "rejoice." What David prayed for in Psalm 38 he gave thanks for in 30:1. By restoring David to health, God made it impossible for David's foes to enjoy his demise. For this, as well as for the healing itself, David gives thanks.

Including the Community (Psalm 30:4–5)

Invitation

Giving thanks was an individual experience in Old Testament worship but it was not a private experience. Typically, as is the case here, the individual worshiper would invite others to join in the celebration of thanks. Here the "godly" are invited to join in. The "godly" in Hebrew are the *khasidim*. This is the word from which we get the adjective Chasidic (also spelled Chassidic, Hasidic, and Hassidic), used in reference to a very conservative branch within Judaism. In the Psalms the *khasidim* are the faithful ones (18:25) or the loyal ones (132:9). They love God (97:10), trust God (86:2), experience God's forgiveness (32:6), and strive to live in keeping with God's will (85:8).

They join with all of creation to thank and bless God (145:10).

The verb translated "sing" is used both for singing and for playing musical instruments.[6] The verb translated "praise" is *hodah* ("to give thanks"). Taken together, these verbs show that the worshiper is inviting the godly to join in the celebration of thanks by joining in with the singing of songs of thanksgiving.

How wonderful to experience God's restorative power! How wonderful to have others share in our joy and gratitude to God as we share with them what God has done for us! We know this from our experience, and we are taught this from the songs of thanksgiving.

Motivation

The motivation offered by the worshiper to the community can be summarized in three words: inevitable, incomparable, reversal. To underscore the theme of *reversal*, which will be picked up again in 30:11, the psalmist sets forth two contrasts: anger versus favor and weeping versus joy. The psalmist experienced a dual reversal. God's anger was replaced by his favor, and weeping was replaced by joy. This shows us that God's anger and favor are not just attitudes within God but are also actions by God. The psalmist understood his illness to be an outworking of the anger of God,[7] which resulted in the psalmist's weeping, and his healing as an outworking of the favor of God, which resulted in the psalmist's joy.

The two sides of each contrast are not, however, really comparable. They are in fact *incomparable*. The poet teaches us this with another contrast: moment versus lifetime. Compare one brief moment in your day with the entirety of your whole lifetime. No comparison at all! That, says the psalmist, is what the experience of God's favor is like in comparison to his anger. No comparison at all!

The poet draws out one final contrast to teach us the *inevitability* of our experiencing God's favor resulting in our joy: night versus morning. No matter how long the night may feel, the morning always comes! Over the last several years my family has often driven straight through from Florida to Pennsylvania to visit family. The middle of the night is by far the hardest part of the trip. No denying that realty. But the morning always comes! That is the point! You may be "in the middle of the night" in some area(s) of your life right now. Hold on, says the psalmist, because the morning is surely coming for you. As surely as morning replaces night, joy will replace your weeping. It is inevitable. It must, because the greatest reversal has already taken place when God the Father drew Jesus up out of the well of death and hell. That reversal took place for you and is already at work within you (Romans 6:1–11).

Is it still the night for you? Have hope, because "joy comes in the morning"! Has the morning already dawned for you or for others around you? Give thanks, because "joy comes in the morning"!

Recounting the Details (Psalm 30:6–10)

Presumptuous Spirit

At some point in the past, David was experiencing "prosperity." The Hebrew word translated "prosperity" is *shalwah*, which is used to refer to times of ease, rest, and security.[8] Two keys give us insight into its meaning in 30:6. One is the beautiful figure of speech that follows in 30:7:

> Your favor, O LORD, made me as secure as a
> mountain.

In our day we would say, "Lord, your favor made my life like the Rock of Gibraltar." Hebrew *shalwah* refers to a time of ease and rest that results from great security. For David that security was no doubt all-encompassing. It would have included things like military and political security, physical and financial security, and emotional and spiritual security. The all-encompassing nature of this security is confirmed by the second key. In 122:7 we read this prayer:

> O Jerusalem, may there be peace [*shalom*] within
>   your walls
> and prosperity [*shalwah*] in your palaces.

Here the poet pairs *shalwah* with *shalom*, a word used for success, prosperity, personal and public safety, and welfare.[9] *Shalom* is used in a comprehensive way to describe a state of wholeness where *all* is well.[10] The prophet Isaiah paints this beautiful picture of *shalom* for us:

> The palace and the city will be deserted, and busy towns will be empty. Herds of donkeys and goats will graze on the hills where the watchtowers are, until at last the Spirit is poured down upon us from heaven. Then the wilderness will become a fertile field, and the fertile field will become a lush and fertile forest. Justice will rule in the wilderness and

91

righteousness in the fertile field. And this righteousness will bring peace [*shalom*]. Quietness and confidence will fill the land forever. My people will live in safety, quietly at home [*shalom*]. They will be at rest. (Isaiah 32:14–18)

Shalwah likewise refers to this time of prosperity when all is well (Jeremiah 22:21). Such a time is what God has created us for and has redeemed us for. This is what David was experiencing and this is the deep desire of our own hearts.

With 20/20 hindsight David saw that this prosperity was the outworking of God's favor in his life:

> *Your favor*, O LORD, made me as secure as a mountain.

But in the moment David lost this perspective:

> When I was prosperous I said, "Nothing can stop me now!"

A more wooden translation of David's sentiment would be, "I will never be shaken" (see the NASB, ESV, and NIV). A spirit of humility and gratitude for God's favor was now replaced by a presumptuous spirit.

Such presumption blocks the flow of God's favor into our lives. So David said in 30:7, "You turned away from me." Humility opens the channel of favor and lets it flow fully. As the ancient proverb says:

> The LORD mocks at mockers,
> but he shows favor to the humble. (Proverbs 3:34)

The New Testament version of this proverb says:

> God sets himself against the proud,
>   but he shows favor to the humble. (James 4:6)

Presumption had transformed prosperity into adversity. Instead of being well, David was ill.

Cry for Help

Prayer is often the first sign of a renewed humility. In 30:8–10 we have a record of the prayer that David offered to God in his adversity. In this brief prayer David did two things. First, he asked. In particular, David asked for "mercy." "Mercy" envelops David's prayer:

> I begged the LORD for mercy. (30:8)

> Have mercy on me. (30:10)

The word translated "mercy" is *khanan* and often has the sense of showing generous kindness to those in need:[11]

> The wicked borrow and never repay,
>   but the godly are generous givers [*khanan*].
>   (37:21)

> The godly always give generous loans [*khanan*] to
>   others,
>   and their children are a blessing. (37:26)

David was asking God to be kind to him in his need, and he was asking for a generous portion of this kindness.

David was asking to be restored to *shalwah* in general and to good health in particular.

This is clear from the second thing that David did in his prayer: he motivated. In 30:9 David basically said to God, "Keep me alive because I am no good to you dead." At the ultimate edge of death David used an ultimate argument to persuade God to keep him alive. David understood that ultimately he had been created to praise God. He had been created to glorify God and to enjoy God in this life. Simply put, if David were dead, David could no longer praise God. God would gain nothing from David's death. In fact God would loose something valuable. God would loose the songs of thanksgiving being sung among the worshiping community. God would loose the testimony to the good things he had done in drawing David up from his grave illness.

This kind of motivation offered to God sounds rather strange in the ears of modern believers. This is probably the case for many reasons, but chief among them may be a purely heavenly orientation to our hope. It is easy for modern believers to think so much about the ultimate rescue that takes us to heaven that we loose all hope for rescue in this life. As we saw in the last chapter, however, the theology of the Psalms is very much oriented to this life (see chapter 3, page 56). As David said elsewhere:

> Yet I am confident that I will see the LORD's
>   goodness
> *while I am here in the land of the living.* (27:13)

It is this same perspective that lies behind David's prayer in Psalm 30. David understood that God highly values this life and not just the life to come. Since God does, David did. Since God does, we can. And David thought God's high valuation of this life might sufficiently motivate God to keep David alive. David was right! God reversed David's circumstances and restored him to full health. David celebrates this reversal in 30:11–12.

Celebrating the Reversal (Psalm 30:11–12)

Reversal Revisited

As in 30:5, so in 30:11 David uses several contrasts to celebrate God's reversal of his circumstances. The first is "mourning" transformed into "dancing." The Hebrew word translated "mourning" (*misped*) expresses much more than sadness. Hebrew *misped* refers to deep, deep grief. Such mourning is often coupled with weeping (Isaiah 22:12) and wailing and howling (Micah 1:8). In fact, the NLT at times translates *misped* with "wailing":

> And as news of the king's decree reached all the provinces, there was great mourning among the Jews. They fasted, wept, and wailed [*misped*], and many people lay in sackcloth and ashes. (Esther 4:3)

Hebrew *misped* is used to express the deep grief experienced in the face of death:

> Now my people, dress yourselves in sackcloth, and sit among the ashes. Mourn and weep [*misped*] bitterly, as for the loss of an only son. (Jeremiah 6:26)

95

> When they arrived at the threshing floor of Atad, near the Jordan River, they held a very great and solemn funeral, with a seven-day period of mourning [*misped*] for Joseph's father. (Genesis 50:10)

"Mourning" is thus an apt description of David's emotional experience during his "grave" illness.

"Dancing," on the other hand, is associated in the Old Testament with great joy (Jeremiah 31:13) and laughter:

> Again you will take up your tambourines and go out to dance with the those who laugh. (Jeremiah 31:4, my translation)

Dancing is often done to the accompaniment of singing and the playing of musical instruments:

> Praise him with the tambourine and dancing;
>   praise him with stringed instruments and flutes!
> (Psalm 150:4)

What a reversal! The deepest of griefs transformed into the highest of joys!

The second contrast is closely related: clothes of mourning replaced with clothes of joy. "Clothes of mourning" is literally "sackcloth." Sackcloth is a rough cloth typically made from camel hair, goat hair, hemp, or flax. Wearing sackcloth would be like wearing burlap. The physical discomfort of the sackcloth made it an appropriate external symbol of the internal discomfort associated with mourning. Thus the wearing of sackcloth was often associated with mourning:

They shave their heads in grief because of you and dress themselves in sackcloth. They weep for you with bitter anguish and deep mourning [*misped*]. (Ezekiel 27:31)

One cannot be literally "clothed with joy" (Psalm 30:11). This is an example of the figure of speech called metonymy: the substituting of one noun for another with which the first is closely associated. So a newspaper headline might say, "White House Issues Statement," where "White House" is a figure for the President of the United States, the head of the executive branch of the government. Literally David would have been wearing fine, festive garments as he went to the sanctuary to celebrate God's rescuing him from the verge of death. Such festive garments would have been worn on occasions of great joy, so the poet says, "You have . . . clothed me with joy." What a reversal! Burlap replaced with party clothes! He who had one foot in the grave now celebrates as one full of life.

Gratitude Given

Singing—not silence—is at least part of the purpose of God's rescuing David from his grave illness. When ill, David motivated God to rescue him, arguing that were David to die he could no longer praise God in the land of the living by telling his story to others (30:9). The first half of 30:12 probably means, "that I might praise you here in the land of the living rather than descending into the silence of the "grave." This same verb for "silence" is used in reference to the grave in the very next psalm:

Don't let me be disgraced, O LORD,
for I call out to you for help.

> Let the wicked be disgraced;
> let them lie silent in the grave. (31:17)

God yielded to David's motivation and rescued David from the realm of silence so that David might sing God's praise among the living.

So grateful is David that he is not content to sing one song of thanksgiving as the fulfillment of the vow he made when he was ill. There is no thought of minimum fulfillment of obligations at this point. He who has been delivered much gives thanks much.

David closes his song of thanksgiving with a pledge to be grateful "forever." When we read "forever" in the Psalms, we think of "throughout all eternity." Most of the time, however, "forever" means something like "for a long, long time" or "for the rest of one's life." A clear example of this sense of "forever" is the phrase *servant forever*, which the NLT rightly translates as "servant for life":

> But suppose your servant says, "I will not leave you," because he loves you and your family, and he is well off with you. In that case, take an awl and push it through his earlobe into the door. After that, he will be your servant for life. (Deuteronomy 15:16–17)[12]

For the rest of his life David will tell his story to others. He was gravely ill. He cried out to God for divine intervention. God responded by restoring David to full health.

The final note in this psalm is a note of praise and thanksgiving, just as the final note of the entire Book of Psalms is a note of praise:[13]

Let everything that lives sing praises to the LORD!
Praise the LORD! (150:6)

Though you may at times feel hopeless in the darkness of life's adversity, the truth is that you always have reason for hope. Thanksgiving and praise always get the last word! Though weeping may go on throughout the night, remember: *joy comes in the morning!*

For Further Reflection
Representative Songs of Thanksgiving

Psalms 18, 30, 34, 40, 41, 66, 92, 116, 118, 124, 138

NOTES

Chapter 1: Songs for the Journey: Genre in the Psalms

1. Richard N. Soulen, *Handbook of Biblical Criticism*, 2nd ed. (Atlanta: John Knox, 1981), 75.

2. Walter Brueggemann, *The Message of the Psalms* (Minneapolis: Augsburg, 1984).

3. Rarely do the authors of the Gospels record Jesus' exact words. Most of the time they give us his words in translation. Jesus taught in Aramaic, but his words are recorded in Greek. When we read Jesus' words in English, we are reading an English translation of a Greek translation of what Jesus said in Aramaic. See Mark 5:41 and 15:34 for two places where Jesus' words are not translated into Greek but are passed on in the original Aramaic.

4. See Tremper Longman III, *How to Read the Psalms* (Downers Grove, Ill.: InterVarsity, 1988), 21–23.

5. See 3:1 for "psalm" (*psalmos*), 6:1 for "hymn" (*hymnos*), and 4:1 for "song" (*ode*).

6. Longman, *How to Read the Psalms*, 68.

Chapter 2: What a Wonderful World! The Songs of Praise

1. The NLT reads: "You allow them to produce food from the earth—wine to make them glad, olive oil as lotion for their skin, and bread to give them strength." The word translated "food" in 104:14 is the same word translated "bread" in 104:15 and is a common word for "grain," which was used as "food" in several ways, including "bread." The sequence of grain, wine, and oil is common

101

in the Old Testament, because the harvest of these three basic food crops was grain, grapes, and olives (Deuteronomy 7:13; 11:14; 2 Chronicles 32:28). The sense of Psalm 104 at this point is that God provides grain, wine, and oil—the three basic foods that give strength to people.

2. Mark D. Futato, *Transformed by Praise: The Purpose and Message of the Psalms* (Phillipsburg, N.J.: P&R, 2002), 7–10.

3. The first four words of 103:1–2 and last four words of 103:22 are identical in Hebrew (*barekhi nafshi et-yhwh*). An echo of this matching can be heard in the NLT: "Praise the LORD, I tell myself" and "As for me—I, too, will praise the LORD." The Hebrew is actually a command addressed to the self; see the discussion at the end of the chapter.

4. The Hebrew word *hod* is translated many ways in the NLT, "honor" and "splendor" being just two.

5. Also see 45:3, where the NLT uses "glorious" and "majestic" to translate this pair used in reference to the human king.

6. For a more detailed study of the image of light in the Bible, see Leland Ryken et al., *Dictionary of Biblical Imagery* (Downers Grove, Ill.: InterVarsity, 1998), 509–12; and William P. Brown, *Seeing the Psalms: A Theology of Metaphor* (Louisville: Westminster/John Knox, 2002), 81–103.

7. Mark D. Futato, *Creation: A Witness to the Wonder of God* (Phillipsburg, N.J.: P&R, 2000), 3–8.

8. Ibid., 43–63.

9. Psalm 104:19–23 is an example of the synopsis/resumption-expansion technique used by Hebrew authors. See Herbert Chanan Brichto, *Toward a Grammar of Biblical Poetics: Tales of the Prophets* (Oxford: Oxford University Press, 1992), 13–19. An author will first give a brief synopsis and then resume the point and expand upon it in the following verses: synopsis, moon (104:19a) and sun (104:19b); resumption-expansion, nighttime activities (104:20–21) and daytime activities (104:22–23).

10. Darkness and night are frequently used as negative images elsewhere in the Old Testament (see, e.g., Job 3:6; Psalm 139:11; Micah 3:6).

11. Mark Futato, "A Meteorological Analysis of Psalms 104, 65, and 29" (Ph.D. diss., The Catholic University of America, 1984), 93–94. See also *TLOT* 2.590–602.

12. See Futato, *Creation*, 1–10.

13. Christo H. J. van der Merwe et al., *A Biblical Hebrew Reference Grammar* (Sheffield, England: Sheffield Academic Press, 1999), §19.4.3(iii), and *IBHS* §34.5.1a.

14. See *NIDOTTE* 1.759.

15. See *NIDOTTE* 1.764.

16. Futato, *Transformed by Praise*, 7–10.

17. Ibid., 7.

Chapter 3: O Lord, How Long? The Songs of Lament

1. The Book of Psalms as a whole exhibits this same movement from plea to praise, from suffering to glory, as does the life of Christ. For more on this see Futato, *Transformed by Praise*, 11–25.

2. The English tradition of using "Lord" (written in small capitals) is rooted in the ancient Greek tradition that uses the word *kyrios* ("lord") to render God's personal name. The Greek tradition is itself rooted in the ancient Hebrew tradition that substituted the Hebrew word *adonay* ("lord") for God's personal name, so as to avoid misusing the name, as required by the third commandment: "Do not misuse the name of the Lord your God" (Exodus 20:7). *Kyrios* is also the Greek word used in the New Testament in reference to Jesus Christ. To confess that Jesus is *kyrios* ("Lord") is, therefore, to confess that Jesus is the God of Israel.

3. This connection is a frequent theme in the Book of Proverbs and in the Psalms that share wisdom themes, like Psalm 112: "Happy are those who fear the Lord. Yes, happy are those who delight in doing what he commands. Their children will be successful everywhere; an entire generation of godly people will be blessed. They themselves will be wealthy. . . . All goes well for those who are generous. . . . Such people will not be overcome by evil circumstances. . . . They will have influence and honor."

4. This is not to say that life has no mysteries, as in the story of Job. It is to say that not all times of trouble are Job-like in character.

5. John Calvin, *Commentary on the Book of Psalms*, trans. James Anderson (Grand Rapids: Baker, 1979), xxxvi–xxxvii.

6. "Want" used to be used regularly for "lack," as in "the wealthy want for nothing," meaning "the wealthy lack nothing." This meaning of "want" is now rare in everyday speech.

7. Here the verbs in English as in Hebrew are imperatives, which are often used to give commands. In Hebrew, the imperative is regularly used to make a request (*IBHS* §34.4b).

8. The Hebrew word is regularly translated "succeeds." In ordinary English, "succeed" is a broader term than "prosper," a term that is usually restricted to finances (Futato, *Transformed by Praise*, 70–75).

9. See *IBHS* §16.3.2e.

10. For the second verb, a cohortative, used for firm resolve, see *IBHS* §34.5.1a. For the first verb, a jussive, as the equivalent of a cohortative in this case and therefore used for firm resolve, see *IBHS* §34.1b.

11. A wooden translation of the Hebrew reads, "The desire of a man is his unfailing love." Most translations interpret this to mean, "What is desirable in a man is his kindness" (NASB; compare NLT and NKJV). While this certainly is a possible interpretation of the Hebrew construction in question (*IBHS* §9.5.2f), I think the NIV is correct, because the consistent sense of "desire of X" has "X" doing the desiring rather than being desired (Psalm 10:3, 17; 21:3; 112:10; Proverbs 11:23; 21:25; Isaiah 26:8).

12. See *IBHS* §30.5.1e: "perfective of confidence."

Chapter 4: Mourning to Dancing! The Songs of Thanksgiving

1. See *NIDOTTE* 2.406, *TWOT* 1.365, and *TLOT* 2.503.

2. Several psalms use *hodah* to express thanks to God for what he did in the distant past (e.g., Psalm 105–7, 136). This reminds us that we are studying poetry and not algebra. Descriptions of genre are generally true, not mathematically precise.

3. See *HALOT* 4.1695–96, *NIDOTTE* 2.406, and *TWOT* 1.365.

4. Thirteen other psalms have historical notes: Psalms 3, 7, 18, 34, 51, 52, 54, 56, 57, 59, 60, 63, 142.

5. The verb is from *khayah* ("to be alive") and is in the piel pattern, which here means "to keep/preserve alive" (*HALOT* 1.309).

6. *HALOT* 1.273–74 and Francis Brown, S. R. Driver, and Charles A. Briggs, *A Hebrew and English Lexicon of the Old Testament* (Oxford: Clarendon, 1953), 274.

7. The Book of Job teaches us that not all illness is the outworking of God's anger.

8. *HALOT* 4.1505.

9. *HALOT* 4.1506–10.

10. *HALOT* 4.1509.

11. *TWOT* 1.302.

12. See also 1 Samuel 27:12 and Job 41:4.

13. Futato, *Transformed by Praise*, 15–20.

Index of Scripture

109

Mark D. Futato (M.Div. from Westminster Theological Seminary; M.A. and Ph.D. in Semitic languages and literature from the Catholic University of America) is professor of Old Testament at Reformed Theological Seminary, Orlando campus. He previously was associate professor of Old Testament at Westminster Theological Seminary in California.

His in-depth study of the Book of Psalms has spanned over twenty years. During that time he has taught the Psalms both on the seminary level and in church seminars and classes. Mark and his wife, Adele, have known the transforming power of the Psalms in the midst of intense personal struggle.

He has also written a major commentary on the Psalms and was part of a team that translated the Psalms for the New Living Translation. In addition, he is author of *Transformed by Praise: The Purpose and Message of the Psalms, Creation: A Witness to the Wonder of God*, and numerous articles on Old Testament studies and the natural world.